TEN STUPID THINGS
DR. LAURA

TELLS WOMEN
TO DO TO MESS
UP THEIR LIVES

MS PEARL

TEN STUPID THINGS DR. LAURA TELLS WOMEN TO DO TO MESS UP THEIR LIVES

MS PEARL

Copyright © 1998 by MS PEARL

ISBN 1-892896-54-0

Published by:

PUBLISHING.COM

519 West Lancaster Avenue
Haverford, PA 19041-1413
Info@buybooksontheweb.com
www.buybooksontheweb.com
Toll-free (877) BUY BOOK
Local Phone (610) 520-2500
Fax (610) 519-0261

Printed in the United States of America

Printed on Recycled Paper

Published March, 2002

PREFACE

Judge not, that ye be not judged.
For with what judgement ye judge,
Ye shall be judged: and with what measure ye
mete,
It shall be measured to you again!

Matthew 7:2

My hope is that this book will help both men
and women to decide for themselves which path
in life to take, without the help of one whose
path has not been stellar.

ACKNOWLEDGEMENTS

I have a lot of "little people" to thank. This book is a compilation of letters sent to me on my Web Page that I started in 1995 and other information I collected from other sources on the Internet. My Web Page was entitled "Dr. Laura Is Wrong". You will find part of that Web page in the back of the book. I got so much traffic on my Web Page, I decided that I had no choice but to write a book and get this information out to the public. The information I collected is from people all over the world who listen to Dr. Laura's show. Some agree with her views but the majority of the people whose comments appear in this book believe that her views are antiquated and in the past, as do I. The past is gone never to return. We have to live for "Today".

Most people believe that her style is abrasive and offensive and should be labeled as "ENTERTAINMENT ONLY".

I am not a talk show host. I am not a psychologist, psychiatrist, or therapist but I know that people have the power to use their own minds to make life choices. They do not have to be led down the path of "Righteousness" by someone who is less than "righteous".

CONTENTS

INTRODUCTION

Dr. Laura Schlessinger has hit on the SCAM of the Century. With family values becoming the theme of the political agenda in the late eighties-early nineties, Dr. Laura has picked up the ball and is running with it. Her show is simply a product of conservatism, which has become popular with the American people at this time. She is represented as the conservative answer to religious talk radio. Her stance on most issues is that of right wing, rich, conservative, white Americans.

Dr. Laura is the host of a daily three-hour internationally syndicated talk show. I was compelled to write this book because of the bad advice Dr. Laura gives to callers of her show. She bases her answers on her personal religious beliefs rather than using what she learned in her years of training.

I started listening to Dr. Laura when she replaced another popular talk show host in a late nighttime slot on KFI that I enjoyed. At that time she was a much better person. The fame hadn't gotten to her head and her answers were direct and to the point, but she was not the cynical and rude person she is today. That was many years ago. I continued to listen because her show was entertaining and humorous.

It gave me a laugh while I worked on my computer, which I did very late most nights. I was amazed at the stupidity of the people who called in for her advice. Then I started to hear all of the bad advice she was giving to people who called in need of her help.

Then Dr. Laura became "RELIGIOUS". She began to demand that people change their "EVIL" ways and live according to her personal religious beliefs. She started to preach everyday about the way God wants people to live. All of a sudden every caller was doing something immoral or ungodly. The first question for every caller became "Do you believe in God?" "Do you go to church?" The answers became "You need to spend some time in church." "God can help you solve your problems." "You must have faith in God." "You need to have some socialization with other people who believe in God." When someone calls her in emotional pain, she says to him or her "What do you think God put you here for? To suffer!!" I thought this was supposed to be a radio talk show with a highly trained therapist – not a religious program. When I found this letter, it fit so perfectly I had to put it in the middle of this paragraph.

Letter:
"I believe that the reason for so much religious talk is because the context of Dr. Laura's show is based on religion now. That's one of the first things I hear. Hardly a caller would go by without the person's religious views asked, "Do you belong to a religious organization?"…"Have you talked to your pastor or rabbi?"… Why does this need to be such a large part of the person's question/answer time on the phone? They called to get her opinion, not a holyman's.

A few years ago the show was based more on the CLINICAL evaluation, not a religious aspect. (Anyone out there remember?) I had been a listener for several years, but it seems to be the same dance with each caller. I am just making an observation, not a criticism; don't get me wrong, I am very happy that the DOCTOR found happiness with her religion, but not EVERYONE can share her religious enthusiasm. We are all so different with different influences and family traditions.

The religious inquisition may be a way to get her audience to analyze what's in their heart and soul, but the clinical way made people make decisions with their MINDS. I hope some day the old show format will come back 'round…even though this format has attracted a lot more attention to the show…I wonder if there are others like me who have 'fallen off' the Dr. Laura bandwagon? (end)

Disagreement is allowed in the real world, but not in Dr. Laura's world. No normal, healthy person would ask for her help. It is unfortunate that those who are least able to protect themselves are also those most likely to seek help from this kind of fraudulent therapist. Dr. Laura likes people she can pick on. Her callers are all carefully screened and you will never hear anyone challenge her. Life's situations don't have simple equations to solve them. Each human situation is complex and needs special consideration. She is using her radio show and callers problems as a platform for pushing forth her own agenda. She is also making a living making "SHOCK RADIO" out of people's lives.

Dr. Laura has also tapped in on the upcoming millennium, during which man's yearnings for peace, freedom from evil, and the rule of righteousness upon earth are finally realized through the power of God. Will the world end in the year 2000? Some people believe so. It won't be the end, but it might be the end of the world as we know it. People are becoming fearful about those changes. They are not sure what will happen in the future and many have turned to religion to relieve their anxiety. Sensing the anxiety, Dr. Laura is capitalizing on people's fear and insecurities and those who want to go back to the "Good old Days". The "Good old Days" were only good, however, if you were male and white. Dr. Laura is trying to drag some contemporaries back into the time of oppression for blacks, women, and other minorities, including Jews. Her desire is to re-introduce the Victorian shame concepts of the 50's by using terms like "shacking up", "knocked up" and "slut". Her show is not only abysmal, but it teaches unrealistic concepts.

She has however marketed herself well!

My book, unlike Dr. Laura's books and her radio show, is a compilation of many, many opinions, not just mine. On Dr. Laura's show there is NO discussion. Dr. Laura NEVER accepts input. When someone has a legitimate disagreement, she cuts him or her off and talks over them until she can transition into another call. My ultimate dream is to be in a one on one discussion with Dr. Laura.

If you'll remember, Dr. Laura only became "RELIGIOUS" 3 or 4 years ago. Dr. Laura is listed as a member of the editorial board of the Skeptics Society. This is a science and reason group that supports a scientific viewpoint of all matters including religion. This view is totally at odds with the orthodox religious faith that Dr. Laura claims to hold.

It is hypocritical to be an orthodox Jew and a member of an organization that questions the existence of God. She has changed her agenda to fit the climate, as is her style. Her show was not originally the moral showcase it is today. She did not receive international fame until after she changed the format of her show to that of a religious one.

As we all know, Dr. Laura has not been a saint in her not so distant past. She has lived with a man she was not married to, she has had an affair with a married man, she has had an affair when she herself was a married woman, she has had sex outside of marriage, she has broken up a family, she has taken pornographic photos, and she has been an atheist. Dr. Laura is NOT without sin.

CHAPTER ONE
TEN STUPID THING DR. LAURA TELLS
WOMEN TO DO TO MESS UP
THEIR LIVES

1. LIE TO YOUR TEENAGE DAUGHTER ABOUT THE FIRST TIME YOU HAD SEX.

2. LEAVE TOWN IF A MAN IS THREATENING YOU.

3. DON'T HAVE AN ABORTION - HAVE THE BABY AND GIVE IT UP FOR ADOPTION.

4. NEVER SPANK A CHILD, THAT'S CHILD ABUSE.

5. YOU ARE IMMORAL IF YOU SEND YOUR CHILD TO DAY CARE.

6. YOU ARE IMMORAL IF YOU HAVE SEX BEFORE YOU ARE MARRIED.

7. YOU ARE IMMORAL IF YOU LIVE WITH A MAN BEFORE MARRIAGE.

8. PASS UP A GOOD EDUCATION AND RAISE YOUR CHILDREN.

9. STAY IN A BAD MARRIAGE FOR THE KIDS SAKE.

10. QUIT YOUR JOB AND STAY HOME WITH YOUR CHILDREN.

Plus 1

MEN - QUIT YOUR JOB AND GIVE UP YOUR FINANCIAL STABILITY AND MOVE TO WHATEVER CITY, STATE, COUNTRY THE WOMAN WHO HAD CHILDREN WITH YOU MOVES TO.

1. LIE - Dr. Laura told a woman to tell her
teenage daughter that she got married on a
different date so the daughter would not know
that she was pregnant when she got married. To
me, that is telling a lie. On the other hand,
Dr. Laura said this quote: "If a parent is not
telling the truth, you're not going against the
parent. You're going against a lie. And you
always should do that no matter who it comes
from. You should never stand by a lie just
because you want to stand by the person telling
the lie." I don't think a mother should ever
lie to her children about anything. A parent
has to give that respect to get it from their
children. Kids learn by example.

Dr. Laura,
     Shame on you. You should know a lie is a
lie, no matter what! I'm surprised you
actually told somebody to tell one. I listen
to your show, but now I doubt your judgment
concerning different things. Oh well, I'm just
disappointed that you ENCOURAGE people to lie.
TSK, TSK, TSK.

2. LEAVE TOWN - Dr. Laura always tells women to
   run away and hide if someone has threatened
   them. On the other hand, she said this
   quote: "Anything you have to run away from
   is your master. If you want to be a slave
   to your fears of inadequacy in handling
   these questions, you will drive yourself
   nuts." I think women should take a
   different course of action. I think women
   should defend themselves. When you run away
   from a bully, he continues to torment you.
   When you stand up and defend yourself, nine
   times out of ten, the bully goes away.

3. ABORTION - Abortion is not for everyone but as long as it is a legal procedure in this country, who is to determine whether it is right or wrong except the person who is in that position? Since the laws of this country are based on society's morality, abortion can not be deemed an immoral act.

Letter:
        I have heard how Dr. Laura feels about abortion, and sex education, but I have not heard her stand on overpopulation. Seeing however, that her stands tend to indicate to me at least that she wouldn't think that there was an overpopulation problem, I would ask her to explain Easter Island. (end)

        Another aspect of the abortion issue is that Dr. Laura always tells women "Don't have an abortion - have the baby and put it up for adoption". Dr. Laura seems to believe there are millions of families just waiting to snap these children up. She says on the air "I can announce that there is a baby to be adopted and I will have the phones flooded with people wanting to adopt it". Dr. Laura does not take into consideration the race of the child. Adoption statistics show that black, hispanic and mixed race children are virtually impossible to place. These children end up spending their lives either bouncing from foster home to foster home or stuck in a group home until the age of 18. They are then turned out into the world and expected to take on family relationships of which they have no life experience. They have never seen or been a part of a real family for any length of time.

Here is a paragraph from an article that I sent to Dr. Laura about the adoption of children of color: Of course it got no mention on the air.

People are often surprised to learn about the disproportionate number of children of color there are in this country waiting to be adopted. More than 60,000 boys and girls are growing up without a family. African American children make up 46.3 percent of the children in foster care, nearly three times their representation in the general U.S. population of children.

3. SPANKING - If spanking a child is abuse everyone I grew up with should be a serial killer. Spanking an immediate, effective form of discipline that works. It does not teach children to be violent; it teaches them that there are limits, which are not to be exceeded. Too bad society doesn't teach this concept to adults. After I started to write this book, Dr. Laura got religious and her views on spanking changed. I guess she read the scripture that states, "Withhold not correction from the child, thou shalt beat him with the rod." I decided to leave the subject of spanking in the book to show how Dr. Laura turns with wind.

Letter:

Truly, there is a difference between spanking as discipline and abuse. Abuse comes from anger and wanting to 'teach the kid a lesson'… spanking comes from love and the desire to have the child LEARN a lesson. Sometimes, especially at young ages, it's the

only solution that makes any sense. My 2-year-
old, if put alone in her room, will tear it up!
If put in a corner, she doesn't stay...and I have
a 4-year-old who invariably needs something as
I'm watching guard over said corner. Holding
her with her arms tightly at her sides...forget
it! I read to do that once and thought, hey, I
have nerves if steel. I can do this. Well,
thirty-five minutes later we were still sitting
on the couch, her all but blacked out from
screaming, me calm as could be but coming to
the realization that this was NOT a working
solution!

Now, when she gets into a blinding fit,
the only thing that works is to spank her. I
don't count to ten, I give no warnings. She
is told to stop, and if she does not, she is
spanked. She cries for about 5 minutes after
the spanking, but then wants hugged – go
figure! Something about having gotten to the
point that warrants being spanked, and then
having it happen, almost makes her yearn for
the 'making up' with Mommy. Five minutes. It's
over. And the tantrums are far and fewer than
they ever were before this policy took effect.

I once heard someone say that they think
time-outs are more painful for everyone (in
comparison with a spanking)...their premise was
that a time-out lasts longer and puts kids in
sadness for more time than swats. With swats,
when they're over, they're over. They are every
bit as much to be avoided as time-outs, if not
more so), but they do not rely on enforcements
for the rest of the day. They get swats, they
cry, they want loved on, and then everybody
goes about their business...and the child tries
to avoid having it happen again. With some
children, spanking is the only way to gain and
regain control.

4. DAY CARE - Day care is a very acceptable
   alternative for parents who want to work or
   can't afford to stay home with their
   children. Not everyone has that option. It
   does not make you immoral or selfish. It's
   just what has to be done in some
   circumstances. I took great pleasure in my
   career. I did not want to stay home. I
   wanted to work. I was a single parent but
   if I had a partner, I would have also
   worked. It is not fair for one person to be
   burdened with all of the financial
   responsibility of raising a family. Today,
   two paychecks are needed just to survive.

Letter:

     Dr Laura stated on 9/6 that since we don't
see animals leaving their offspring to others
for care, then we as humans should take the
hint and care for our own offspring as well. If
the animals "think" it's important then so
should we.

     However, she isn't completely truthful (I
happen to think it is ignorance) with her
statement. There are NUMEROUS examples
throughout the animal kingdom in which mothers
and fathers leave their offspring to others for
temporary care. (We all know that in most
animal groups the males contribute almost 0% to
the care of offspring but that's another
story.) Before you say, well those are just
animals and we are different keep in mind that
Dr. Laura wanted to use animals as an example
that we should follow. So she can't use the
argument that we should be like them when it's
convenient (the moms/or dads should care full
time for the babies) and then change and say we
should be different when she finds out that her
argument is not supported by the data.

Examples of animals who regularly use helpers to raise their young include: honeybees, scrub jays, hedge sparrows, mongooses, baboons, lions, and primates to name a few. In some of these cases (scrub jays and honeybees) the helpers are related to the parents but in other groups there is no blood relationship. In addition, there is evidence that the amount of time mother birds spend with offspring decreases DRASTICALLY after the first week or few weeks of life.

The message is there is VARIETY in the animal kingdom. Not all animals brood their young as Dr. Laura implied. Cowbirds don't brood their young at all. They depend solely on other species to incubate and rear their offspring – a bird day care! We also find many other vertebrates including primates like us who depend on helpers to raise their young (sounds like daycare I think). Gee, maybe daycare isn't an original human idea after all!

The above info is presented in many undergrad bio curruculums. Dr. Laura's degrees are in biology/physiology, not therapy.

5. SEX BEFORE MARRIAGE – This is really a hard one considering all of the STD'S today. However, Dr. Laura was not a virgin when she married the first time and I know she had sex with her present husband before she married him. Therefore, she is not in a position to address this issue as she has. She had her fun and now that she is old and has religion and a microphone, she wants to put restrictions on other people's sexual activity. My mother had this saying, " DO

AS I SAY, NOT AS I DO"! I guess Dr. Laura
lives by the same saying. I know this is a
cliche that has been around forever but would
you buy a pair of shoes before trying them on
first or how about buying a car without a
test drive? People need to be compatible
sexually. Why find out after it is too late?

Letter:

Dr. Laura is way too extreme about many
things. I also find her to be very narrow-
minded, old fashioned and unrealistic. She
believes that ideally people shouldn't get
married before the age of 28, give or take a
few years. They also shouldn't live together or
have sexual intercourse. I know that she is
talking about the ideal situation but she is
fifty, is married and can have sex whenever she
wants. I am 24 and have a boyfriend of about
four years. We will probably not get married
for at least 3 more years due to financial
reasons. We DO have sex. We use protection and
are very careful. If I were to become pregnant
we would likely marry earlier than we planned.
I realize Dr. Laura is trying to lead people
down the right path but it is much easier for
her to preach after she has made all of her
"mistakes".

6. LIVING TOGETHER – As far as I know, what
consenting adults do is their personal
business. I know a lot of elderly couples
who choose living together because if they
were to marry both their pensions would be
cut in half. Dr. Laura says it shouldn't be
about the money, but sometimes that's a very
important factor. It is not shameful or
immoral as Dr. Laura preaches, just another
option if you want to be with someone but
don't want to be married.

Letter:

I would not marry a man until I lived with him. You need to experience and know everything you can about the person you are marrying. You need to know how they wake up, if they leave pantyhose in the shower, if they leave the seat up, if they drop clothes on the floor and if they mind if you use their razor. If you can't live with this person, it's better you find out before, not after you are married. I disagree with Dr. Laura that it is immoral. I think it's a very smart thing to do.

7. EDUCATION - A woman should do everything she can to better her lot in life. Education is the key to being able to provide children with the things they need to survive. It also gives women pride and security. In knowing that their mother is educated, children know that they will still be provided for if any circumstances arise, (Divorce, death of a father, etc.), which are beyond the control of the family. Dr. Laura is always bragging about her extensive education. Other women deserve the same opportunities she has afforded herself.

Letter:

Dr. Laura told some poor single mom that she shouldn't go back to school and better herself because it would mean her 9-year-old would have to be left with a sitter. When the woman said she wanted to get a better job and provide a nice home for her son, Dr. Laura told her to rent a room in a boarding house because it doesn't matter where they live, so long as the mother is with her child. Let's see Dr. Laura come out of her mansion in Malibu or whatever ritzy suburb she lives in and practice what she preaches. Ivory towers are nice places, aren't they?

8. BAD MARRIAGE - A marriage that is not healthy and happy (a lot of fighting) one is no place for children to be. It is much better for a child to grow up in a single parent home that is peaceful than to deal with an arguing, fighting, unhappy two parent home. I've heard many kids say, "I wish my mom and dad would get a divorce. All they do is fight."

Letter:

I see I'm not alone in thinking Dr. Laura is narrow-minded. What concerns me most is her stand on parents staying married for the sake of the "covenant" and the kids. When my husband and I got married, we took the covenant of salt…we would rather die than divorce. We had two children early in the marriage who are the joy of my life. Even after getting counseling three times, we still were unable to enjoy Christmas, a drive to the beach, or even a meal without his yelling and criticizing. Many times the kids left the table without eating to get away from him, and by mid-morning on Christmas Day, they would be crying because Daddy was yelling again. With much apprehension and guilt about breaking the covenant and the family, after 15 years I gave up on the marriage and persuaded him to leave. The first Christmas that he was gone, my kids said it was the best Christmas they had ever had. Now you tell me that it is better for the kids for Mom and Dad to stay together. It's one thing if you are both willing to try, but one person can't do it alone, and it isn't fair to put such a burden of guilt on someone who is making the heartwrenching decision to do what is best for the kids and himself/herself, even if it means "kids never get what they want" (a quote from Dr. Laura, that kids want both parents). What a kid wants is two parents living in peace, not two parents hating each other's guts and screaming at each other. The next best thing is one parent who puts the child's needs first and gives him a peaceful home.

9. QUIT YOUR JOB – Most financial situations do not allow for a woman to "quit her job" and stay home with the children. Children, especially daughters need the example of a mother who contributes to the world as a role model. This gives them the confidence that they can be an independent adult and take care of themselves in the future.

Letter:

I deeply regret that you feel the way you do about working moms. I am a working mom who works HARD to put a roof over my boys heads. I work HARD to feed them and clothe them. I do not work for "the fun of it". I sure wish that I could. But I cannot. And it's very unkind of you to seemingly group all working moms together and sterotype us as bad because we work. It's offending that you think we should stay home and "love and raise" our children. I can't stay home. I wish I could, but if I quit, I would have to apply for welfare and sponge off of the other hard working people of

America. Not that welfare is evil or anything,
it's just NOT a lifestyle. Being dirt poor is
not a lifestyle. I have a middle-class, two
paychecks, paying high tax family.

Now, I can't condemn at home mothers. I am
a working mom that envies them. How nice they
have it to spend every moment with their
children. If my husband gets a BIG raise, I
will drop my job like a sack of hot rocks!

I do not understand why other people
condemn us. Is it envy? Is it the lack of
self-esteem?

My first son is having a hard time at
school. When the teacher calls me to come get
him for unrulyness, YES I go get him, but on
my lunch break, so as not to burden anyone
else with my job tasks. It's a simple thing
called time management.

In closing, please don't condemn working
moms. There is a reason for working and
reasons to stay home. Just different strokes
for different folks. I know how strong your
beliefs are and I am glad that you stick to
your guns, but I just had to ask why you so
vehemently condemn working moms.

Plus 1

I have heard Dr. Laura on many, many
occasions tell men they could not accept a job
in a state other than the state that the mother
of the children he fathered live in. I have
also heard her tell men to quit their jobs and
follow the woman who has his kids to whatever
state she decides to move to. I wonder how Dr.
Laura thinks these men are supposed to make a
living. Where are they supposed to live? How

are they supposed to support the children they are quitting their jobs to follow around the country? What if the woman moves to a state where the economy is not great? Jobs are not easy to come by. When challenged on this she says "You fathered these children, it is your responsibility to do whatever it takes to be wherever your child is. If that means you have to give up your job and move, then so be it". .

I heard Dr. Laura tell a man with four children to quit his day job and get a paper route at night so he could get custody of his children from his wife. A paper route. "You can make a living doing that", she said.

It is also Dr. Laura's belief that a young girl should not spend the night at the house of a friend if the friend is being raised by a single father. When I heard her say this, I did not know where she was going with that statement. I could not think of a reason why she would say this. Then she said, "A young girl should not be running around in her pajamas in front of her friend's father. If there is no woman in the house this is unacceptable." I was shocked! I could not believe she said this. Is she now stating that all men who raise their children without a woman in the house are pedephiles and child molesters? Would she not trust her husband to be in the house with an eight-year-old girl in her pajamas if she were not there? I had several men friends who were raising their children in the same neighborhood that I lived in when my children were growing up. There was no hesitation in letting my daughter spend the night at a friend's house because there was no mother in the home. My daughter was not molested by any of her friend's fathers. How bizarre this woman's thinking is. I never really considered Dr. Laura a man basher until I read her book "Ten Stupid Things Men Do To Mess Up Their Lives". Now it is confirmed, Dr. Laura is definitely a man basher.

Letters:

#1

Dr. Laura

You repeatedly recommend that the custodial parent not take a transfer if it moves the kids away from the other divorced parent. I think you discount too much the value of the job to the family welfare.

#2

Dr. Laura,

Today you got on a man with two girls in his custody who had to move for his job. A good paying job is not worth giving up or easy to get. If they were still married, his wife would have relocated. Get real! It's not always wise to cash out just to stay in the same town with the ex wife and kid's mother. For a divorced man to quit his job, when he has custody and expenses are greater than if he were married and not continue to care for his kids and career would be stupid.

#3

Dr. Laura,

I just heard your opinion and I felt I just had to write. Story -- divorced man with custody of two girls, one 15 who knows mother committed adultery and the other child who is 8 and does not know. Man moved to another state because of his job. You placed the blame for splitting up the family on the man.

1. The wife's actions split up the family.
2. The man is providing for the family.
3. If they were still married, the wife is expected to follow the husband if it doesn't conflict with her job, which she had none.
4. I feel you missed the mark on this one.

In the beginning, I thought I was the only one who disagreed with Dr. Laura's views on Day Care, Working Mothers, Spanking, Marriage, Religion, Abortion, and her overall attitude and harsh judgement of other people. Through my research, I have discovered there are many, many other people who feel the same way I do. There is a lot of criticism and resistances from much of our society who disagree or even ridicule her staunch position on morals and values. Dr. Laura doesn't have the right to make value judgements for anyone other than herself.

CHAPTER TWO

DAY CARE / WORKING MOMS

In my research, I found Day Care and Working Moms to be the most controversial subjects I encountered when talking to people and searching the internet for people who also oppose Dr. Laura's views. I set up a web page and it gets plenty of traffic. Putting down Day Care and Working Moms were the biggest areas where people expressed their disagreement.

Day care is an alternative that has been used for years to take care of children while parents worked. Josephine Marshall Dodge founded the first Day Nursery in 1888 in New York City. She was hoping to show that the Day Nursery could serve the goal of instilling middle class values into working class children. Obviously, Day Care has been around for a very long time. In 1893, Mrs. Dodge demonstrated a model Day Nursery at the Worlds Columbian Exposition in Chicago. In 1895 she founded the Association of Day Nurseries in New York City. In 1898 she founded and directed the National Federation of Day Nurseries, which grew to 700 members in 20 years. Why is Dr. Laura trying to change a tradition that was started over 100 years ago? She states that this is a new trend that only started in the 70's with the Women's Liberation Movement.

Sure, there are bad Day Care providers, but you find bad people in every profession. That does not stop us from using other professional services. Good professional Day Care is available if one does the research it takes to find the right place for your child. It's not an easy task and can be very time consuming, but it is doable.

This is a quote from Dr. Laura. " A long time ago I made the comment that if you cannot afford to be there and take care of your children, you ought not have them. I got righteously attacked for that. And I came back with let me understand something. If you can't afford two cars, who let's you take the second one home? Somehow the concept when it's an inanimate object is better understood than when it's a human being." There is no comparison to the way you get a baby and the way you get a car.

Dr. Laura promotes books with titles like "IF YOU CAN'T MAKE TIME, DON'T MAKE CHILDREN" and Domestic Tranquility - A Guilt-Free Guide for the Stay-At-Home Mom. Who is Dr. Laura to make the rules for anyone else's life decisions? In the first place, well over 50% of children are not planned. Birth control is not 100% effective. If you have sex on a regular basis, you will eventually end up pregnant.

Not everyone can stay home and care for their children. For most women staying home is not even an option. Most women work outside the home because they have to, not for "pin money" or some abstract notion of self-fullfillment. There are many single parent homes for many different reasons. Divorce, the death of a spouse or in some situations there was never a marriage but there is a child.

Dr. Laura thinks this is a terrible thing.
While I agree that it is not the ideal
situation for a child (nor for a parent) to be
in, it happens. When it does happen, and it
does happen a lot, we have to deal with it. To
be perfectly frank, more children are born out
of wedlock than within the bonds of marriage.
There has never been a time in our society when
women didn't have children without being
married and there never will be. Where does
Dr. Laura think all of the people who are
looking for their birth mothers are coming from
who were born in the 50's and 60's?

       There was never a time in our society when
women didn't go to work and leave their
children in the care of others. Women before
us did it and women after us will do it also.
Just because Dr. Laura had the luxury of
staying home to raise her son, she has no right
to tell women that they are bad mothers and
immoral people if they can't afford to stay
home with their children. Dr. Laura was almost
40 years old when she had her child. Most of
us "normal" women who have no trouble getting
pregnant have our children when we are in our
twenties. Does that mean women who have
children in their twenties should give up the
next ten to fifteen years of their life to
raise a child? Dr. Laura tells women to sell
their homes and move into a small apartment so
they can stay home with their children. She
also tells women to get rid of that second car
and sacrifice everything that is considered (by
Dr. Laura) to be a luxury to stay home with
their children. Most of us don't live in the
lap of luxury to begin with. With today's
economy as it is, in most families it takes two
paychecks just to make ends meet. It is very

expensive to raise a child. The price for
clothes, food, and providing the basic
necessities is enormous. Dr. Laura says kids
would rather have a mom at home than to have
decent clothes to wear to school. I beg to
differ. Kids are so cruel today. If your
children go to school in second hand clothes,
they will be tormented. I don't believe in
"Keeping up with the Jones", but I do think you
should provide the best you possibly can for
your children. If that means both parents
working, then so be it. I wonder how many
times that Dr. Laura sent Deryk to school in
second-hand clothes.

A sociology study in 1984 found that women
most likely to be hospitalized for depression
were full-time housewives and mothers.
Housewives are also more likely to use alcohol
mixed with other mood altering drugs. A 1973
research on drug use revealed housewives were
more likely than working women to use
tranquilizers, barbiturates, amphetamines,
controlled narcotics and antidepressants.
Other studies indicate that anywhere from
twenty to thirty percent of housewives use
psychoactive drugs on a regular basis. Women
who identify wholly with this role are certain
to face problems because being a housewife and
mother is not a lifetime job. Husbands leave
at a very high rate, leaving women to fend for
themselves and their children. Husbands also
die, sometimes prematurely. Even if the
husband remains in the home children grow up
and leave. Many women find themselves with
empty nest syndrome. Fifty years ago a woman
had only a few years to live after her last
child was married. Today the average woman
spends forty-one percent of her adult life

without children at home and at least twenty-three percent with no husband. A woman who makes the wife-mother role the core of her existence is both out of a career and an identity.

The average woman is assigned primary responsibility for the care of her young, usually within a nuclear family structure that leaves her totally alone with her children most of the day. Our society considers this ideal. The roles of men and women are not simply opposite sides of a coin - they are fundamentally unequal. Men can not keep their dominant place in society unless women remain in a dependent place, i.e. no job. In a man's world, good women are primarily concerned with the needs and welfare of others.

Dr. Laura is trying to mold women into becoming a perfect paper doll cut out in man's image. Women who live within the limits of the roles assigned to them by men are sometimes rewarded by a degree of approval from men. This sometimes cushions them from the reality of their subordinate status in society. It often keeps them from recognizing that the status exists. When a woman complies, her reward is economic security. However, this is not always the case. Most women who have faithfully carried out their prescribed duties of being a housewife and a mother are discarded by men who tire of them and replace them with younger women. These displaced housewives are often reduced to living and raising their children on welfare. With limited job skills and earning power, these women will never rise above their present status and remain on welfare. If you go to work to provide for your children, you are a bad mother for not staying home with them. If you stay home with them and accept assistance, you are lazy. Due to men's general unwillingness to support women when they no longer care for them, they will also not be provided for in old age. Because the woman has not worked and accumulated social security, she will not have a retirement fund which means living at or below the poverty level for the rest of her life.

I was totally overwhelmed by the amount of response I got on these two subjects. Here are some of the letters I received on my web page and picked up from other sources on the Internet.

DAY CARE – WORKING MOM LETTERS

#1

My mother worked full time yet found the time to attend every open house, field trip, dance recital, concert, etc. My grandmother watched us during the day and we lacked for NOTHING. We grew up successful, well adjusted, and self-sufficient. We didn't get pregnant, do drugs, or be with "bad" people. She knew all of my friends, their parents, and she knew where I was every minute. If I said I was going somewhere, she would check to see if I got there. My husband, on the other hand, came from a family where his mother didn't work. He also is well adjusted and happy. I have no children, however if I did, I would still work. College doesn't pay for itself. Neither does retirement, and I would not put my husband into an early grave forcing him to be the sole source of our income. It just isn't fair. We are a TEAM, which means equal contributions, financially and otherwise. When I was growing up, several of my friends lost their fathers due to divorce or death. Their mothers were totally lost. They had no job skills, didn't know how to balance a checkbook, but yet had to find a job. Very difficult indeed. I was always thankful for my mother and very proud of her. Some men like to have their wives at home. It gives them the feeling of power. Keeps them in their place, so to speak. Other men are proud of their wives and what they've accomplished. Whatever works for each couple is what works. There is no right or wrong. There is good day care and bad. Staying at home does not guarantee being a good mother. There is good and bad in both instances.

#2

I have read lots from stay at home moms about how involved they are in school activities. That has NOT been my experience. I am a working mom and was a Cub Scout leader for 4 years. All the other leaders - (with 1 exception) were also working moms. When I would ask stay at home moms to help, I was usually told that "they would love to but did not have the time." What are they doing with their time? If working moms can fit Cub Scouts into their schedules, why can't stay-at-home moms? I think that working moms are in general better organized than stay at home moms and can therefore fit more activities into their day.

#3

As a young married couple who would like to start a family, (especially being a woman), I hear all these educated, career oriented women who can't wait to stop working to stay home with their children. After a year the most these women can offer is a 10-minute speech on why J&J baby wipes are better than Luvs. Please! Get a life. Just because you have children doesn't mean you have a life. In some cases it's the opposite.

You can also see the changes in the relationships with their husbands. Bowing to every demand. It's pathetic. They feel they can no longer have an opinion about the finances and wait every week for their allowance. PLEEEEEEEASE!

#4

Stay at home mom's do not like generalizations made about them. Well, working moms do not like it either. I do not believe that all stay at home moms are boring but I also do not believe that all working moms are selfish and do not have close families, and have screwed up kids. In fact, the worst kids I know are from families where the mother stayed home with them. If you can't stand the heat, stay out of the kitchen. If stay at home moms dislike generalizations so much, quit using them about working moms.

#5

When I was growing up, I always valued the time I had at home alone. My mother always worked part time, and starting at age 9, I got a key to the house and had an hour alone with my younger brother before both my parents came home.

Even at that age I valued time to myself, and I think that some parents forget that their children are different from them and that their achievements not those of their parents. Often, when my mother was at home, she felt she had to be doing something for me when I was in a bad situation, although I did not want the help...often I could not enjoy an achievement because it was not "mine".

I shared some of my minor triumphs and crises with my parents, but I kept some of them to myself. I doubt many adults with healthy lives tell their parents everything...this can't magically happen when a child hits 18. A bit of separation is necessary for all but the youngest children.

I became an adult, and now live on my own, manage my own finances, and take care of myself. I think that if my mother had not taken some "selfish" time to herself, I would not have been able to learn to depend on myself...not only for the "important" things, but to learn to amuse myself, to work out some of my own problems, and to be without a hand to hold.

We can not have independent adults if we do not require children to learn responsibility. Even at a young age children do not need to have someone kiss every boo-boo. After a child is school age, they should learn to first try to slay the smaller dragons, and then go for the help that is always there.

#6

I work full time, I'm in the Air Force, and I have 2 children, a 3-½ year old daughter, and a 15-month-old son. Stopping my career and picking it up later was not an option for me - there is no "leave of absence" in the military. I respect the choices made by women who choose to stay at home, but it would be nice for a change to have them show some respect for those of us who work outside the home. No two people are the same, and it is ludicrous to believe that what is best for one family is best for all families. My children are the center of my universe, but they are not my entire universe, I don't think that would be healthy for any of us.

#7

I'm a Dr. Laura nightmare: knocked up at 26 by a man married to one someone else.

My poor, neglected, unfortunate kid is 5, has been reading since he was three and works 4-figure addition and subtraction.

He's already an orange belt in martial arts and sings solos in the church children's choir. He can discuss with you the importance of having faith, patience and being able to forgive. He is a generous, kind-hearted child of God.

He graduated preschool with honors and has interpersonal skills that enables him to settle disputes among peers, apologize to them when he's guilty of a 5-year-old fit of anger or a tantrum and interact gracefully with children from ages 2 to 17. My house is full of neighborhood kids often - boys and girls.

In his head are the telephone numbers to my office, cell phone, home phone, my mother's work phone, and home phone. He recognizes that there are consequences to choices and when he makes a bad one, he's got to face the music. I could go on and on about him, but I'll spare you.

I returned to work when he was 3 months old. I had to since I was guilty of non-marital sex as well as adultery and opted to raise my child instead of choosing the noble act of adoption. I had to fight for child support but the sperm donor has not been a participant.

Yes, my son craves male attention, enough of which he does not receive from my dad, uncle, and brother-in-law, his godfather. I'm not ignorant of the fact that he would greatly benefit from a father's daily influence. I'd happily be home for him when he's done with his kindergarten day if I could be. The circumstances I made for myself precluded that ability. This semester he is in karate class while I attend graduate school.

Working moms vs. stay at home moms, marital child bearing vs. out of wedlock pregnancies—these are valid controversies. I'm making the best of my situation, as are most of us. It's difficult to raise children in the best of circumstances. Those of us who are not in the ideal situations don't need debate.

#8

I am a single mom who is finishing her last year of college, and my daughter goes to day care three days a week, and she loves it. I do not have a problem with stay-at-home moms, but I cannot abide by the other bigoted comments that bash working moms, or daycare. I am planning to be a teacher and I will be home most days at four, or earlier. I will have my weekends off. Dr. Laura should quit picking on others because they do not agree with her point of view.

#9

I think teaching our children to tolerate and accept differences in people are important. The world is made of different people with different viewpoints and we need to teach that what is right for one person may or may not be right for another.

What would YOU (Dr.Laura) do if your child decided to have a family in which BOTH parents decided to work outside the home? Disown your child?

Mspearl

#10

Dr. Laura does not give children enough
credit. Children are very resilient and given
the opportunity to blossom they will do so.
Parents who "hover" over them may stifle this
creativity.

I have seen this in my sister. She has a
son who cries when he is separated from her. I
think kindergarten and elementary school will
be especially difficult for him. He is
accustomed to her being there 24/hrs a day and
7 days a week. I personally don't think that's
healthy.

#11

I have wanted to write in for ages to
point out that the "stay at home mom" trend is
a VERY recent trend. My father talks with
great admiration about his grandmother spending
her day working the farm side by side with his
grandfather. Their oldest daughter took care
of the house and the other kids, and grandma
reports that the minute these kids were big
enough to hold a hoe, they were out working
too! What? No infant stimulation programs?
No moms continually doting-making them feel
like the center of the universe? There wasn't
time. Of course, all six of my great-
grandmother's children grew into hard-working,
productive adults. Amazing.

#12

We live in economically volatile times.
Downsizing, strikes etc. A family with only
one income puts themselves at tremendous risk
unless they have a tremendous savings account.
It often takes a downsized individual a year or
more to find comparable work. Meanwhile,
someone who has been out of the work force
often needs retraining or recertifying and
can't just jump back in on a minute's notice.
True, one can bag groceries and earn enough to
eat but health insurance is tremendously
EXPENSIVE. If you have little children, going
without this insurance for any length of time
is irresponsible. Relying on the government,
extended family etc., when you have refused to
work, is unfair. My husband and I both work
and have comparable, but modest incomes. Our
budget is set up so that we live on only one
income. This way, a job loss means we could
meet our regular bills as usual. We will
continue to provide this measure of security
for our family. Financial problems are the
leading cause of divorce. We owe our children
intact families.

#13

Working parents can be "their kids mom or
dad." You have said that loving children is
not enough and truer words were never spoken.
We must love and nurture as well as provide
support (financial and emotional), guidance,
and time for our kids. Many adults, whose
parents worked long hours to build a future for

them, treasure the moments and memories they have of time spent with and sacrifice made by those parents. Life is about service, children learn and respect this message from parents, whether a parent is at home with them all the time or spends treasured hours with them before or after work. The commitment to children and family does not end at kindergarten, but children must be nurtured, loved, guided and spent time with through childhood. Would that we could learn to respect all parents doing their best to serve their children and raise them to be strong, healthy, happy and moral adults willing and able to serve others they encounter in life.

#14

My mother and father BOTH worked full time. My grandmother took care of us when we were not in school, until mom came home. Guess what? We lacked for NOTHING as far as guidance, support, encouragement, and love. I was principal violinist in my high school, in the top 2% of my class of 581, danced ballet, tap, and all that stuff until I was 18. Put MYSELF through school (now there's a novel concept!) because my parents couldn't afford it. My sister and I turned out just fine. We didn't get into trouble, didn't get pregnant, and none of that stuff. Just like you. So that proves that good people can come out of BOTH working and non-working mother homes. I am very proud of my mother because she taught me independence, not dependence. I too am very successful in my career, wouldn't give it up for anything.

So we can agree to disagree. There is no
"right" way. Each family is unique. I've seen
a lot of druggies and "bad" people come from
so-called "traditional" families.

#15

I'm hesitant to call Dr. Laura because I
feel like she'd get hung up on some of my past
mistakes. Not all of us are in a position to
give our kids what we think they deserve (mommy
at home). We do what we have to in our own
unique situations.

#16

My son was born and I stayed home with him
for 18 months. It was hard and I thought a lot
about going back to work to escape the
responsibility. It was also wonderful and I
enjoyed every minute.

My husband and I hit a financially
devastating period and I had to go to work. I
loved working and felt completely miserable
everytime I dropped my son at daycare. I think
you are making it difficult for parents to feel
good about the decisions they make. With every
choice there is a trade-off. I don't know
whether staying home or working is the best
thing for me. I do what I have to for us to
survive.

#17

In the past, children were at home with their mothers - ladies who were contributing to the well-being of the family in ways that are generally done by providing increased income in our current society. Women gardened - today they earn money so they can BUY produce. Women used to sew clothing - today they earn money so they can BUY clothing. The children did see them contribute, because societally, this was the way things were, and technologically, nothing more was possible.

I love my microwave. I love my can opener. I would not want to go back to the days of the washboard. But I don't think we can legitimately ignore the fact that children watching and observing their mothers work was of great benefit. Today, whether at home or at daycare, all to often the day is spent playing? Today, because mom and dad are both bringing home the bacon, the basic needs of the child are so easily met that his responsibility is primarily to himself and his own things. I suggest to you that a daycare in which children play and learn to get along with other children is not necessarily the best place for a child, but these kind of activities can build character and a sense of responsibility. We want to have it all. If the road to having it all means both parents working, then so be it. Put the kids in daycare, because having the nice stuff money can buy is important today. They'll learn to get along with other children.

#18

I'm a working mom. I have always been a
working mom, and will never give up my career.
Neither will I ever give up my "mom-hood"
because my proudest and greatest accomplishment
is my three brilliant, beautiful, talented,
successful children. I'm not going to argue
with anyone about whether I did the right thing
about going to work when they were little. I
struggled with the guilt, and still do, and
yet, when I look at them and see what they are
doing, listen to their plans for their futures
and share in their special times, I know I made
the best choice for MY family. I know children
of full time moms who are screwed up beyond
belief. I know children of working moms who
are strong, independent, capable, moral
religiously observant, and contribute at least
as much back to their community as they receive
from it. But I am wise enough to know, and
understand from my knowledge of statistics,
that it is dangerous to generalize to the total
population from a sample of 1 (Dr. Laura's
kid). Each side has it's own set of
sacrifices, and each side has it's own way of
making things work.

#19

I would venture to bet that most 2-income
families NEED the money. Dr. Laura doesn't
seem to think so but then when was the last
time she had to worry about paying a bill.
Since she pulls a 5-figure salary for a single
speaking engagement, I doubt that money is an
issue for her. Many of us need two incomes to
have a modest lifestyle. I, myself, would not
prefer to live on welfare.

#20

It seems to me that most of the bombing is criticizing the working parents. WHY IS THAT? We don't see working parents attacking stay at home parents. Why are stay at home parents so critical of working parents? In my humble opinion, if you have time to sit around and bitch about other people who are honest hard working people then you have TOO much time on your hands.

#21

If you want to stay home, nobody is telling you not to. That is YOUR business. If you want to work, that is also YOUR business. College doesn't pay for itself, neither does the mortgage/rent, food, clothing, and retirement. Social security will probably NOT be there in 20 years, and then people will whine because they don't have enough money to live on. Well, whose fault is that? There is no written law that says if you have kids that you have to be poor or "financially challenged". Kids grow up just fine either way. There are good and bad parents who stay home just as there is good and bad that work. Dr. Laura has a twisted misconception that working couples go out to dinner every night, drive Mercedes and shop at Nieman-Marcus. Well, get real and wake up. The cost of living varies throughout the country. A $30K income may be sufficient for some small one-horse town, but in many places it is almost welfare wages. Housing costs $1000 just for rent in

many parts of the country, usually where jobs
are plentiful. Or maybe you would rather see
people live off the government? Then on the
other hand tell them to cut welfare to the
bone? You can't have it both ways. Like I
said. If you want to stay home and play the
martyr, then fine, so be it. But DON'T YOU
DARE criticize something you know nothing
about! Very Christian indeed, aren't you?

#22

Your slam of working parents is bigoted.
Very few working parents with whom I am
acquainted can afford new cars, annual
vacations, and frequent dinners out. Most
spend the majority of their non-working hours
involved in activities with their children—i.e.
sports, homework, etc.

Could many working parents reduce their
lifestyles, get by on one income, and spend
more time with their kids? Sure, but before
you cry "selfishness!" think of this: None of
us really need more than a mud hut to live in
and a couple of meals a day to survive. Isn't
it selfish to sacrifice any time with your kids
to rise above this level? Why not have your
husband quit work also and go on welfare so
that you could both spend 24 hours a day with
the children? If welfare doesn't appeal to
you, I'm sure your family could make enough
money scavenging aluminum cans to get by. Sure
you might have to give up water and
electricity, but what's more important? Get a
grip, people need to work!

#23

Don't get me wrong, I'm not trying to put
down stay at home moms but some animals have
day care. We live on a ranch and I have
observed our cows dumping their young off on an
older cow to watch, just so they can eat in
peace and chew their cud without being bothered
by their calves. Thought you could get a laugh
out of this. I could send a picture of this if
you want.

#24

Some parents don't have the choice of
staying home and being their "kids mom." It is
not the matter of a new car, etc. My husband
and I are farmers and with the price of land,
taxes, and food going up, and the price of
small grains going down, how are farmers
supposed to even exist? We BOTH either need to
have outside jobs, or better yet, let's have
the price of grain stay compatible with the
current cost of living. I would love to be a
stay at home mom and so would almost every
working mother I know. But, we need to feed
our children. Talk about being between the
devil and the deep blue sea...if people like
you feel this strongly about working mothers,
PLEASE let our Congressmen know. We farmers
are less than 2% of the voting public. Who do
you think our legislators are going to listen
to? Farmers? NOT!!

#25

It appears to me that stay at home moms
think it is okay to do: outside activities,
volunteer work, and maintain hobbies that would
mentally stimulate them and provide them an
extension from which they can express
themselves and enrich their own lives. If this
is true, please explain to me WHY Dr. Laura has
been so critical of women who choose to fulfill
these same desires through a job. Volunteer
work that has received such high praise also
takes time away from a child in the same way
that a job would. If you disagree with this
then you have a HUGH LEAP of judgement.
A volunteer job can take 40 hours a week
if you want it to, just like a job can. The
flip side of this is that both volunteer work
and jobs can take less than 40 hours a week.
Those who are being critical of working moms
have not stopped to ask how many hours/week
they work. Most assume the children are in day
care 10-12 hours/day. That's a pretty big
assumption. Many of us work full time but have
flex hours so that our children are in day care
only 3-4 hours/day on selected days.

#26

It is narrow-mindedness like this that
causes a lot of problems in this world!! We
are a dual income family NOT because we want a
new car (our newest is 8 years old.) In fact,
the only time either of us owned a new car was
before we were married. I feel cheated!
Where's my new car and all those dinners out
and that yearly vacation I'm being cheated out

of? I haven't gotten any of those things since we've been married and had the children. I don't work because I want to, believe me. Ask any of my co-workers how many times I have lamented that if I could only stay home with my babies!! In fact, absolutely NONE of the women here at work that have children at home are here because they want to be. I am constantly on the watch for something I am capable of doing from my home so that I can be a stay at home mom. Until then I will have to do what I have to do. Please, please stop making generalizations. Instead, why not lobby for legislation that will reduce the tax burden on the family so that more of us could stay at home and let unemployed men out there have these jobs. Working moms are not greedy and self centered?

#27

Where is it written that all-dual income parents put their children into day care for 10-12 hours a day? Why is it that you make this Hugh leap of Judgement? There are some of us who DO need dual incomes. Example: Some of us have one or more parents, who are not healthy, can't afford their own health care, and need financial assistance. Does this mean I should suffer so that I can stay home full time and take care of my children? I think NOT. Children should be taught priorities!!!! Children are NOT the ONLY priority in a REAL family!

#28

   I think that the friction between
employed/non-employed mothers only increases
with the insults that have been thrown around.
On both sides of the issue there are many
misconceptions. I think that we should support
each other, not drag each other down.

   The mothers that stay at home with their
small children in general work very hard, but
there are the few that don't. On the flip side
many mothers that are employed outside the home
work very hard to make a good life for their
children when they get home and ensure that
their children are well loved and cared for.
So you see, no matter which side of the fence
you find yourself there are no absolutes. We
need to take each other based on our own
motives and behaviors.
   I recall hearing a Native American saying
to the effect that you can not understand
another person until you have walked a mile in
his moccasins. There are those that work to
have nice things. Then there are the rest of
us that work just to help make sure the bills
are paid, food is on the table, there is a roof
overhead and don't have the money for the
extras.

#29

   I have been both a stay-at-home mom and
now a working mom. You can't win either way.
If you're a stay at home mom, you're looked on
as "lazy". When I started working again, I was
up against how can you let someone else raise
your child, don't you want to be the one taking
care of him, and just overall looks. Call me

paranoid but it's out there, especially
listening to Dr. Laura. There is no easy
solution, except plan well, marry rich, or win
mega-bucks. Always love your children and let
them know you are always there for them, if not
physically in their presence in their hearts.
Unfortunately, life isn't as simple as Dr.
Laura makes it out to be. You can't go to the
supermarket and walk out with one bag without
spending at least $20 - $30.

#30

   I would just like to see a mutual respect in
this world. I think certain families do better
when mom is a stay at home person and others do
better when both parents work full time.
Different families have different obligations
and needs.
   I would not presume to say who should do
what. Everyone's circumstances are different.
So why can't there be a MUTUAL respect for both
sides since there should be one common goal -
that of a better society in which to raise our
children and for all of us to have healthy,
well adjusted children.
   I have been on both sides of the fence
(working and staying home). I don't think stay
at home types appreciate the problems of those
who work - they simply dismiss the problems and
say we weren't creative enough. How do you
know that? You aren't there - so don't be so
presumptuous.
   I know many stay-at-home mothers who
really enjoy and can afford to be at home. I
wouldn't criticize them for that. So why
should stay at home types be critical of the
services that working parents provide to them?

There are selfish and untrained children that are raised by stay at home mothers and there are also selfish and untrained children that attend day care. There is no magic solution and not one correct way to raise a child. (Thank God there's not just one correct way to raise a child because if there were we'd have all failed, even Dr. Laura). How many of us were "experts" when we started?

#31

HEAR! HEAR! I can't tell you how sick I am of being beat up and having to put up with all the guilt trips because I am a working mother. I, too, am forced by economic circumstances to work, not because I want to. Fortunately I have a job I like, but I'd give it up in a heartbeat if my husband's income were enough to prevent foreclosure on our house, keep food on the table and clothes on our backs, etc. Neither of us has a new car. We haven't had a vacation in I can't tell you how long. I do what I can to attend school programs, take my kids out for the day, etc. I make each evening a time to spend with them, but Dr. Laura needs to get real. This is the 90's and it just isn't feasible for all families to be one-income families. It doesn't work that way any more, especially in this era of almost non-stop layoffs. I would be happy to stay home with my beautiful children if Dr. Laura wants to pay my bills.

#32

Dr. Laura holds this icon so high; I can't resist giving an alternate point of view.

The full time homemaker and mother as a life partner:

I cannot imagine living with a woman that would abandon life outside the family to raise children. I also cannot imagine myself making such a sacrifice for a woman.

The full time homemakers (mostly female, but there is one male) I have met bore me to death. A line from a song "She married young, and then retired" comes to mind. The longer they are at home, the narrower they become. In time, their children coming home from grade school are more interesting to talk to than the mother is. And then when the husband suddenly leaves her for another woman, she says she never saw it coming. Her children are embarrassed to be seen with her, and she wonders why.

After our children were born, my wife could hardly wait to return to work. She committed 2 years to seeing each child through infancy, but we could sense the effect her entrapment was having on her and the children. And we both saw how things improved when she went back to work.

Advantages in having both partners work:

There is much to be said for bringing daily world experience into the home for both the benefits of the children and the spouse. Be assured that conversation at the dinner table in our house was rich with daily events and news from all members of the family. And mom had more to say than what was on sale at the Pig.

I think children, particularly daughters, need the example of a mother that demonstrates daily contributions to the world. An example of a female that is striving to improve herself, make it on her own. Girls have enough problems with self-sufficiency and self-esteem without being stuck with an adult role model that has nothing else to do but keep the house, cook the meals and catch the soaps in the afternoon.

Reality, though we don't like it, is that spouses die, people get divorced, and the stay-at-home spouse is often thrust into a work-a-day world they do not understand. I think it only makes sense that both parents are prepared and equipped to support the family they have made.

Lets talk about the money. Money is important, extremely important. It is the single most cited reason for divorce. How much you earn determines where you can live, and that usually determines where your children attend school. All things being equal, more expensive neighborhoods have better schools and better facilities. Home computers and the ability to help your children into the best colleges are very critical to their individual success. I am not satisfied to have my children be good people. I expect good, successful people. Thou shalt not be poor should be the 11th Commandment. (I know, being poor is not inherently bad, but it is hard to make it sound like an accomplishment.)

Child Supervision:

Children are better at caring for themselves than Dr. Laura gives them credit for. They can be responsible, and they do learn independence. With the proper guidance and follow-up, a child with a few hours truly to themselves will grow in ways we could not imagine. Granted, we have to be concerned about drugs and bad company, but we must also remember, true imagination and creativity tends to fly in the face of convention. And all we as parents have to offer children is convention, the creativity was drained out of most of us years ago.

Please do not misunderstand me. Maintaining your priorities and making time for your children is critical. They need you, every day. You can't phone in parenthood. You must make time to be together. But it does not have to be 7 day 24 hour coverage. And the children I see that have a parent constantly at their shoulder seem to end up wasting years worried about what mom will think, instead of developing a few skills of their own.

Day Care:

I also challenge the bad rap that daycare gets from Dr. Laura. What makes her think that parents are so competent? All that is required to be a parent is some functioning organs and a little cooperation. At least most daycares have to have some kind of licensing and training. The best of them provide learning and growth experiences that most parents can only dream of. My kids loved daycare and could not wait to go. They both still visit their old teachers from preschool. And no, I was never jealous of the people at this institution.

There have been widely publicized cases of bad daycare centers. But, I hold the parent responsible, you have to know what is happening to your child. The parent that would leave their child at a daycare they had not thoroughly checked out is incompetent. That same parent would not be any better raising the kid himself or herself.

Our grandmothers and great-grandmothers:

I think our forefather's experience bears me out, this idea of the non-working spouse is a very new one. A century ago, when most of us were farmers or shopkeepers, the wife held an important role in the running of the family business. I know my grandmother was milking cows and feeding chickens every day. She participated in any number of tasks about the farm in addition to preparing meals and keeping the house. This was not a woman sitting about doing clever crafts with the kids. This was not unusual, it was the norm. Both husband and wife worked to make a living for the family.

Suddenly, with the migration of workers from the farms to industry, the wife was supposed to become an incompetent stay-at-home sperm receptor, suited only for making babies, preparing meals and running a vacuum. Men still tell jokes about keeping wives barefoot in the winter and pregnant in the summer. I know my mother did not subscribe to this little bit of tyranny. Neither does my wife. And neither does my daughter. Nor my son.

CHAPTER THREE

SPANKING

Dr. Laura stated in the past (before she became religious) that spanking a child was abuse. She has since changed her views on this subject but I have spent so much time collecting information, (I was writing this book before Dr. Laura became religious), I still feel compelled to leave it in the book. The letters quoted here are from people who listened to Dr. Laura when her view on the matter was different.

Dr. Laura quoted "Children are not learning respect for ideals and values because their parents are not living a life supporting those values and because society as a whole seems to be nonjudgmental about bad, self-centered, destructive behaviors." In my opinion, these bad, self-centered, destructive behaviors are a result of children being allowed to get away with a lot of things that a spanking would nip in the bud. I see no problem with a child getting a few swats on the backside on occasion. It kept me in line as a child and it probably kept Dr. Laura in line also. I think all kids need that kind of discipline at some point in their childhood. Child abuse is when more punishment than is necessary is inflicted on a child.

#1

I disagree with your conclusions that spanking is wrong and ineffective. My wife and I have three children. We found that an occasional spanking was a very effective "reality check" for an offending kid in certain situations. We spanked: 1) When we were disobeyed repeatedly on a matter in a short period of time, 2) When flagrant disrespect for a parent was shown, 3) When a child placed him/herself or someone else in danger of serious bodily harm by their actions (playing with fire, etc.). We have found that spanking has become necessary less and less frequently as the kids got older. The kids are all happy, outgoing, and productive and show no signs of becoming tower snipers, serial killers, or attorneys. I think what they learned from the spanking experience was not, as you believe, that it's ok to hit someone to express displeasure but that there are limits which must not be exceeded and that there will be swift, immediate punishment if they are exceeded.

On the matter of withholding privileges: this is fine with an older child. We found out, though, that younger kids have so short an attention span that withholding a privilege for any significant period of time resulted in a series of battles that festered on for as long as the privilege was withheld. A spanking provided punishment that was immediate, not separated in time from the offense, and was also "over" quickly so that things could get back to normal. My opinion is that spanking is both appropriate and effective in certain situations involving younger children, but that other disciplinary techniques become more effective as the kids get older. If you can raise your child to be a productive, considerate, and well-behaved adult without spanking, more power to you. I just ask that you not trash those of us who believe in its judicious use.

#2

I have a six-year-old, a four-year-old, as well as a 21-month-old. I have to admit that there are times when the two older ones are so caught up in what they are feeling and so consumed by frustration that a swift slap on the behind is what it takes to get them refocused.

The spank or not to spank war will rage on, but for my family, it works. I honestly can't remember the last time I spanked my six-year-old because she has learned how to control herself better. The four-year-old is another story! In fact, she got a firm hand on the bottom just this morning!

All this talk about teaching children not to be violent, and then spanking them is hypocritical, is silly. My children know the difference between a spank on the rear and hitting a playmate.

#3

We have a 3-½ year old daughter that we allowed to get way out of control. Instead of following the advice of our pediatrician, a noted advocate on spanking, and instituting a clear, consistent discipline plan (including spanking), our approach was more "by the seat of the pants". We weren't consistent about why and when we would spank, nor did we punish the same offense consistently. We also didn't back each other up - I felt he was too harsh, he felt I was to easy on her. Finally, the discipline problems began to cause a problem in the marriage, which only exacerbated the behavior problems. After a long, calm talk, in which we both expressed our feelings about the problem, we determined that something must be done or this child would go from the small discipline problems to larger ones as she grew older. We discussed the problem with our pediatrician. He discussed some suggestions with us, including spanking, and the plan seems to be working. We have really cracked down on our daughter, and after a few weeks of her being utterly confused about the changes, she now realizes that she is dealing with a united front.

#4

I was spanked, and I feared spanking. However, after I got older I came to realize that spanking was MUCH preferable to longer-lasting forms of punishment.

For the very youngest children, spanking is immediate, and since they reason poorly, they associate the bad behavior with pain. As children begin to reason they think, as I did "Do I want short-lived pain or to be stuck in a corner for an hour?" My father actually gave me the choice a few times and I always chose spanking.

Spanking does not invalidate all other forms of punishment. It actually becomes less effective than other means as your child ages and so needs to be replaced.

Still, it can be effective on an 11-year-old who hasn't been spanked in 6 years and has done something abhorrent! The humiliation was a greater deterrent than any other punishment could have been. I was NOT emotionally scarred and I certainly NEVER repeated the behavior - and was never spanked again.

#5

I am the mother of a 2-year-old. I know it can be frustrating and embarrassing to deal with behavior problems as they creep up. If you believe in non-violent discipline then SO BE IT. Spanking is the discipline choice for most because they feel they have no other alternative, and they are correct. After a child has been spanked everything else is a joke. Have you ever tried to discipline someone else's child who is accustomed to physical discipline? They laugh at time-outs, etc.

People often say they don't want to spank their children but that's what works. It is our job to find what works best for our children to guide them. I have made it a point not to spank, although my child does not obey. I understand child development and don't expect her to. Therefore, I have exhausted every possible avenue to teach her, it is very time-consuming. THERE ARE NO QUICK AND EASY REMEDIES FOR BEHAVIOR PROBLEMS. Our children need time invested into their needs to find a lasting solution.

#6

I'm a grandmother and in the days I raised my children, we spanked. There is a big difference between spanking on the behind and beating a child. I have 4 adult children who have not been permanently damaged by being spanked. They were always welcome wherever we went because they were well mannered and obedient. I don't believe spanking is required for every little infraction, but I do believe that a good swat every now and then, when you need to make sure they understand, doesn't hurt.

#7
It seems to me that discipline has been very lax. I have no problem with a little smack on the butt when warranted. It lets the child know that the behavior will NOT be tolerated. If no discipline is given now, the child will become even brattier as they grow

older. I don't consider an occasional smack on
the butt violent or abusive. Many of our
parents smacked us on the butt when we were
kids, but we didn't grow up to be violent
degenerate people. I see nothing wrong with
it.

#8

I have learned from experience that all
children are different and usually need to be
treated differently. I have been strongly
challenged over the years to come up with
disciplines that work with each individual
child. I have one child that you could spank
all day long and it wouldn't faze her, but she
would do anything as long as I don't put her in
the corner and make her stand still. I have
another child that doesn't mind standing in the
corner, but if I mention cleaning, becomes an
instant angel. My son is the one that
occasionally needs a swat on the rear. It's up
to us to find what works and to be firm and
consistent.

#9

My opinion may not be very popular, but it
is based upon the dynamics of the family I grew
up in. No two children are alike. Some
children are easily disciplined in a "non-
violent" manner. I have found that some
children need a swift kick in the behind once
in a while just to get their attention.
When I was growing up, my father would
spank us and if we were really bad we might get
the "belt". I didn't appreciate it, but I
understand why he did it and I must say those

times I was probably deserving of the
punishment. I do not like to spank my
children, but I have found that, at least for
my family there needs to be a happy medium
between the two extremes. When one of my
children is being belligerent, throwing a
temper tantrum, etc. and I try to communicate
with them to no avail, what I see happening is
they are so caught up in their own situation
that they are paying no attention to me. I'll
try to pick them up and hold them tight with
their arms at their sides to let them know I am
serious and want the behavior to stop. It
doesn't work. At that point they get a swift
pat on the bum.

#10

    As a "Spanker", I don't entirely disagree
with what you are saying. I doubt any thinking
spanker would disagree when you say that
children need to be understood, and sometime
there is an underlying problem to address. On
the other hand, not every misbehavior coming
from a child has some deeper meaning. All to
often, it is simply a result of rebellion or
testing boundaries. I realize that some
"psychobabble" might say that there must be a
deeper reason why they are trying to rebel.
This, I'm afraid, is silly!

#11

Just one question – Have you ever tried to
reason with, **discuss** or **explain** to a 2-year-old
why a certain behavior is not appropriate for a
toddler in the middle of a full-blown tantrum?
Nothing works like a swat on the bottom
followed by a cooling off time. All the
education in the world doesn't take the place
of doing it for yourself. I know, I've done
both.

#12

It is very sad when one person who doesn't
agree with how another is parenting feels she
has the right to snipe, insult, and degrade
another person, simply because she considers
herself more 'educated' in that area.
Secondly, there are many opinions on
spanking vs. not spanking. I personally think
spanking is warranted in certain cases and it
does NOT turn kids into hitters. When my sister
and I were kids, we got a swat on the behind
for serious things. Not for minor disciplinary
stuff, but for something serious, like touching
the stove, or sticking things in the wall
sockets. These activities can cause fatal
injury and a little smack on the butt
reinforced that this was not acceptable
behavior. We were never slapped in the face or
anywhere but our hands or butt. We both turned
out just fine, thank you.
Discipline is lacking very badly in
children today. When I was a child, we were
expected to respect our elders, obey their
rules in their homes, and not touch anything

unless we asked permission. Why shouldn't kids be taught to respect their parents/aunts/ uncles/teachers/neighbors, etc.

Dr. Laura is constantly recommending books for people to read regarding the right way to raise their children. This little poem is a gem!!

JUNIOR BITE THE METER MAN
JUNIOR KICKED THE COOK
JUNIOR'S ANTI-SOCIAL NOW
ACCORDING TO THE PSYCHIATRIST'S BOOK
JUNIOR SMASHED THE CLOCK AND LAMP
JUNIOR HACKED THE TREE
JUNIOR'S SELF-DESTRUCTIVE TRENDS
ARE COVERED IN CHAPTER THREE
JUNIOR THREW HIS MILK AT MOM
AND THEN HE SCREAMED FOR MORE
JUNIOR'S SELF ASSERTIVENESS
IS FOUND IN CHAPTER FOUR
JUNIOR GOT INTO GRANDPA'S ROOM
AND TORE UP HIS FISHING LINE
THAT WAS TO GET ATTENTION
SEE PAGE 89
GRANDPA SEIZED A BELT
AND YANKED JUNIOR ACROSS HIS KNEE
BECAUSE GRANDPA AIN'T READ BUT ONE BOOK
SINCE 1933!!

After reading all of these letters one has to surmise that Dr. Laura is not 100% correct in her assumption that kids have to be home with a parent and not be spanked in order to grow up and become independent, capable, well rounded, intelligent, hard working, self-sufficient, successful, respectful, happy adults.

*Note: Dr. Laura's views on spanking have changed!
The evidence is in this letter.

Although you would think Dr. Laura Schlessinger would practice therapeutic listening, it appears that more often she employs critical listening. That is, of course, when she is not interrupting her callers. Her sense of morals and extreme views of life contribute to her strange approach to advice giving. However, many callers express their admiration for her, and although I feel that she is a terrible corrupting force striving to convert the sheep of society to her own philosophy, if they are entertained by her, then good for them.

If I had a radio call-in show, I would probably approach it in a significantly different way than Dr. Laura. Apparently, her motives are more to present her views on life and the world than to help her callers, as she often disregards their wants and feelings in the dispensation of her advice. Instead of focusing her attention on the caller and demonstrating empathy, as would be required for therapeutic listening, Dr. Laura often passes judgement on her callers and their lifestyles based on the most rudimentary information, taking critical listening to an inappropriate extreme. She reacts critically to many topics, mostly those involving sex. In her place, I would at least try to hear what people are dealing with in their lives before passing judgements.

Dr. Laura's biggest problem seems to be her strong sense of "morals". Although morals in and of themselves are not bad things, taken to the extreme, any viewpoint can be dangerous. Dr. Laura seems to disapprove of sex, coarse language, and lack of commitment in relationships. As soon as one of these items is mentioned in a caller's description of a problem, she immediately interrupts the caller and expounds on their lack of virtue. *The interesting thing about this is that beating children is often recommended by her. When the caller protests, saying there are other ways of dealing with misbehaving children, Dr. Laura will have none of it. Apparently her morals are not stemming from some central assumption on life but are instead decided on a piece by piece basis, with no consistency.*

Dr. Laura's show, despite its fascist sentiments, seems to be relatively popular. Fortunately the AM radio format it uses necessarily limits the show's audience. Dr. Laura may be immanently unqualified to be an advice show host, but if people enjoy her particular brand of fanaticism, then it is okay for them to listen.

CHAPTER FOUR

DR. LAURA, "HOW COULD YOU DO THAT"?

This letter Dr. Laura received from a Future Therapist is the perfect beginning to my chapter on Dr. Laura, How Could You Do That?

Letter:

Dr. Laura,

I have listened to your show and read your column and wanted to share a couple of comments with you about them. First of all, your advice many times is not psychologically sound. In one of your recent columns a reader asked about giving her child a choice on religion by exposing him/her to the various Christian sects. In your reply to her you berated her, telling her that recent studies have shown that it is a bad idea and that people can't be moral without a sound religious upbringing. The study you referred to was most certainly a correlational study, which if you remember any of your psychology courses, you will recall shows no causality. I personally know a multitude of athiest who are more moral than the ministers and priests and a person who was allowed to choose his own religion (as your reader wanted to do), and besides being a right wing republican, he turned out fine.

My second point is you are all too often accusative and rude to the people who call or write. This breaks the first rule of a therapist/client ralationship (this comes from a man who was a therapist for 25 years). A therapist is not to be judgemental nor blame clients for their behavior. I can't believe you were ever a good therapist. The people who like your show are likely those who already have poor self image and therefore anything you say affirms this belief or passives who agree with everything anyone says, either way you are doing them more harm by insulting them and placing blame on them.

Possibly you should go back to graduate school to get some refreshers on how to be a good therapist and learn to be more discerning in the research you quote. Remember that your opinion on how to live life is not the only way or necessarily the correct way (another rule of psychotherapy). (end)

Dr. Laura is a big advocate of following the rules of her religion. She always tells her callers to make peace with a parent with whom the person is estranged. Dr. Laura took a call from a man whose biological mother needed an operation. Because he was mad at her for various transgressions, he did not want to provide the funds for this life-saving operation. Dr. Laura told him that he should provide the funds, because of the Biblical injunction to "Honor thy father and mother". Dr. Laura, on the other, hand is estranged from her mother. She doesn't call her mother to find out if she needs food, medicine or has a roof over her head but that is what she tells others to do. She hasn't talked to her mother for 12 years and she has a bitter rivalry with her younger sister, who has disowned her. Her personal life is filled with conflict and she lacks the ability to evaluate herself.

Another thing Dr. Laura advocates is no sex before marriage. Dr. Laura however, slept with a former co-worker, Bill Balance, on the very afternoon she met him. Dr. Laura also allowed Mr. Balance to take a dozen nude photos of her which have been shown on the Internet. (I saw them). Dr. Laura obtained a temporary restraining order to have the photos removed.

At the time she had the affair and took the photos, Dr. Laura was still married to her first husband. That falls under the categories of sex before marriage and adultery. Dr. Laura also started dating her present husband while he was still married to another woman. She broke up his family. The man was married and had three children with his wife whom he left to be with Dr. Laura. I always hear her say your kids come first, but you can replace your wife. She should know since she replaced his wife. If the child is always the first priority, why did she break up a family instead of doing what she advocates, let them work out their problems and save their marriage. She goes on to say that if the marriage doesn't work out the woman should not have a FUTURE relationship with the man. "If he left his wife and children for you, what makes you think he will not do it to you? Also she says it would adversely affect the children. That woman and her children's lives were torn apart by Dr. Laura's actions. As adults, those children probably have not recovered from the loss of their father and a stable family life. Dr. Laura also lived with her present husband for nine years before they were married.

Everything Dr. Laura preaches, teaches, and nags people not to do, she has done. This is just another case of "DO AS I SAY, NOT AS I DO."

I have also listened to the manner in which Dr. Laura talks down to her callers. I have spoken to many people who also listen to her show and agree that she is rude, condescending, and very short with her callers. Her whistling at people to interrupt them really irritates me. It's very obnoxious and demeaning; people aren't dogs. The biggest mistake that she makes is offering advice before she hears all of the details. These are the people who make it possible for her to have a talk show. I gathered a lot of information on the attitude Dr. Laura portrays on the air as well as in her personal life. People who agree with her views seem to think this is acceptable behavior. I beg to differ with these people. Not even Dr. Laura has the right to belittle anyone. Religious people are not supposed to behave in this manner. (The KKK is a religious organization so I guess it's acceptable to do anything you want to in the name of GOD. That doesn't say much for the religious aspect of things).

I have compiled a series of letters stating the facts about Dr. Laura's attitude toward her callers.

#1

Your web site is like an oasis in the far right desert! I am so pleased to see someone somewhere expose that arrogant, self-righteous, lying, nasty, uppity hypocrite. While listening to her show, and marveling at her cruelty to those masochistic callers who seek the advice of a mean spirited quack, I have noted many contradictions regarding her so-called moral demeanor.

1. She claims that everyone must honor marital vows and not divorce. Yet, she is a divorced woman living with her second husband. This is called adultery in the bible she professes to believe in.

2. She believes in "honoring thy mother and father" but she refuses to speak to her own mother because "there are no loving binds."

3. She believes in the concept of keeping family ties together, yet she refuses to talk to her own sister.

4. She allows various companies to advertise on her program even if those companies contradict her beliefs.

5. The music she plays on her program before each call that has been performed by artists that have had a myriad of events in their lives that have included multiple divorces, out of wedlock children, drugs, alcohol, extra and pre-marital sex. If she were as morally focused as she claims, she would stop playing the music.

6. She had her tubes tied in an effort to avoid pregnancy, which directly contradicts God's teaching that sex is for procreation only. Since she is a divorced woman, and is having sex with her second husband (her former shack up stud) she is, in essence, an adultress.

7. One of the reasons she is on the radio is that years ago, she was "dating" someone who had ties to radio. This person's influence created the opportunity for her to have her own program. In Laura's terms, had this been another person, this could be considered prostitution.

8. Her doctorate, in essence, in "Physiology" makes her a glorified gym teacher. Why does she not have a doctorate in Psychology, or is a qualified Psychiatrist? She is no more qualified to give advice, on a clinical level, than Ann Landers.

9. She espouses taking personal responsibility for one's actions, when she refuses to take her own personal responsibility for the actions she has done in the past. (Her divorce, her refusal to talk to her mother and sister, her nasty and arrogant actions in Dallas, Texas, during a speaking engagement. Instead of owning up to her appalling behavior, she blamed the incident on her "allergies." Had one of her callers called and asked her opinion if the caller had acted the way Laura did, she would clearly have hung that caller out to dry.)

10. She is often rude, nasty, and mean to callers, when she should be sympathetic and kind. She destroys people on the air, when all they need is kindly advice. She kicks people when they are down.

11.   She often blasts feminism and it's so-called destructiveness that has (in her hypocritical opinion) caused society to lose it's "moral compass" when in fact feminism enabled her to have her own radio show. (Because of the societal advances of women, due to the principles of feminism.)

12.   She claims that marriage should be a sacred institution between a man and a woman only. She states that people who choose not to marry should not have the benefits of medical and insurance coverage, of recognition by the government even though they are tax-paying citizens. Interestingly, she opposes domestic partnership laws that would enable gays and lesbians to be recognized as citizens like everyone else and enjoy the benefits thereof. She opposes gay marriages because it's not a man and a woman. So, gay men and lesbians, in her view, have no rights in society even though she claims to be sympathetic to gays and lesbians.

13.   She opposes gay men and lesbians adopting children because she feels a mother and father is more appropriate. Yet, when one caller, a gay man, called and said he was having misgivings of taking the responsibility of a teenage boy (who was in and out of foster care and was clearly in a bad way) she told that caller he must take that boy in with him and his long time partner. This clearly contradicts her stance that gay men and lesbians are not (in her opinion) good parental models.

     I am sure there are many other instances of her contradictory behavior.

#2

Is it only me, or is Dr. Laura snippy and condescending to some of her callers? True, many callers are either not willing to be truthful to Dr. Laura or themselves, but should she be downright rude? I think not.

#3

I think Dr. Laura is snippy—even downright rude—to some callers. Sometimes this is deserved, either because the caller won't get to the point, or is not answering her questions, or is obviously trying to cover up his complicity in the problem he called about; but other times it is not. It seems to me that the incidence of undeserved rudeness by Dr. Laura has increased in the past couple of years. I don't know why this might be, although one obvious possibility is that success is going to her head a bit.

#4

Do you think it is polite to interrupt someone while they are talking, while they are trying to explain and make clear a position they hold but about which they have questions or doubts? Is it polite to take up a gauntlet in the midst of another's platform, and then proceed to carry your own gauntlet instead of giving the attention to the one whom held it first?

What would you do if someone interrupted you and began to ask so many questions that you began to wonder what the original problem even was?

Would you become so confused that the perfectly normal train of thought that you began with would become like a large platter of scrambled eggs, all messed up? Would you like to be asking for assistance, trying to get YOUR point understood, and the person to whom you are speaking goes off on their own tangent, albeit in the same area but in a different direction?

There is only ONE judge and HE will be the one to tell all of us what we have done wrong. Dr. Laura has no authority to invoke her own beliefs on people. Advice is different, that can be taken or ignored. Her radio show is a very interesting model to which to listen. It illustrates the perfectly rude behavior of an intelligent, witty woman. When someone phones her for help, they evidently are desperate or they would go to their local Mental Health Association. Please, study one of your shows, just one time, with an open, accepting mind. Everyone can learn something from his or her own mistakes.

#5

I find myself turned off by Dr. Laura's manner many times and lately I find myself going back and forth between another female psychologist that is on at the same time in our area.

#6 (this letter is from one of her fans who tries to justify her behavior)

Is Dr. Laura obnoxious? Sure. In some ways. She has her bad days. I've heard her when things aren't going well. But tell me, what is more obnoxious, someone who calls it like they see it, or someone who doesn't want to step on anyone's toes, who wants to make everyone their friend, who won't tell you that you need to straighten up? While I do not like to get a swift kick in the butt that often, sometimes I need it, and it does me good. I may call the kick obnoxious, but at least I am getting it.

#7

   I think that sometimes you don't listen to all the person is trying to say before you answer and that frustrates me.

   Get off your moral high horse for one second and think about the people who are calling your show with their PROBLEMS. ARROGANCE BREEDS IGNORANCE!

#8

   Dr. Laura is very obnoxious. I personally believe she could step down off her moral dogmatism and be a normal person every once in a while. For instance, I completely disagree with her notions of judgement on other people. Nobody seems to have the courage to challenge her view. I think we should listen to her with an open mind but also keep in mind that she is human and will on occasion be wrong. It is our responsibility as an audience to think for ourselves and not to hang on every word from one or two people. If we get led down the wrong path it is our own fault and not the show host. We owe it to each other to learn how to think. If we did, we wouldn't need Dr. Laura or anybody else.

#9

I couldn't believe Dr. Laura's reaction to
a man who lived in the country and called and
said that he expects people to take their shoes
off when they enter his home. It frustrates me
that she didn't give him a chance to explain.
He started to say something about the trees
around his house...We never heard the end of
it. It's awful. I'm sorry, but Dr. Laura
rubbed me the wrong way on this one. She is
"city folk" though, so it can be excused as
ignorance.

#10

I have just recently starting listening to
Dr. Laura and I am in awe that she is
considered one of the top 20 influential
people… that is scary. I have heard her
humiliate people, call people names - "hussy",
"slut", etc. I don't understand how there can
be so many desperate people in our society who
believe that one person's view point is the
"right one". I am really surprised she has not
been sued. I am surprised that everyone backs
down to her on the air. I have even heard her
turn the whole story around and confuse the
caller on the issue. Why is she allowed the
freedom to harass people, maybe because they
call her for the harassment? I don't get it,
the woman is sick.

#11

Dr. Laura,

A couple of weeks ago, you told a female caller that it was "none of her damn business" to ask her boyfriend about his past sexual contacts. I would respectfully disagree with you.

In this day and age of HIV, it is ABSOLUTELY a person's business what their partner's sexual history is, especially if sexual intimacy is on the horizon for this person and their partner. That caller's life may depend upon knowing who her guy has been sexually intimate with in the past and she has every right to know it. I think your answer was irresponsible; no longer can a shot of penicillin cure whatever sexually transmittted diseases a person contracts from another. Please consider the ramifications of HIV and herpes and other incurable diseases when you give advice to others on this subject.

#12

Dr. Laura,

Last night on the radio a young girl called who had just lost a school election. She was rightfully upset as other children were calling her loser and they were mean to her. The thing that bothered me was your comment after you found out it was a public school and not a religious private school. First, I believe it was a prejudice and generalized remark as we all can't afford private schools and also not all-public schooled children are rude. If you have children calling in then that means children are listening. You are **sending the message** to them **that private** schooled children are better than public schooled children are. Children do not pick the school they attend, parents do. Maybe you should rephrase that and say that these mean children were not taught respect and courtesy at home.

#13

Why do you care so much what other people do? Your judgemental attitude isn't going to change anyone. If you are so happy, why are you so angry?

#14

When I first started listening a year and a half ago, Dr. Laura's confrontational style made me uncomfortable. It was refreshing to hear someone advocating traditional values so powerfully, but I often found her rude. I also was suspicious that something was rigged. She would jump to an assessment before a caller had finished the first sentence. I figured that either the screener was doing a full assessment off the air and giving it to Dr. Laura in advance, or she was really shooting from the hip. I started to figure her out. She has a set of core beliefs about people's behavior that leads her to catagorize their problems.

#15

Dr. Laura frequently states that many dilemmas are a result of weak character and dismisses ailments like alcoholism, sexual addiction, post-traumatic stress, and others as psychobabble. I have struggled for years with low-grade depression and always thought the only avenue open to me was to pull myself up by my bootstraps (character adjustment) which I did not have the energy for. Recently I've learned there may be help for me with new medications that are available but I'm wondering if, according to Dr. Laura, I'm just weak in character?

#16

I am amazed when I turn on the radio and am made aware of all the people who call up Dr. Laura to be publicly humiliated. When she spent two hours talking to her rabbi after the newspaper articles came out berating her behavior in Texas, did he treat her "personal crisis" like she treats the ones of her listeners? I somehow doubt it. She is not helping people, but rather, making them feel worse about themselves and their problems than they did before they called her. This woman is not compassionate, nor is she a good listener. She depresses me just to listen to her. I am glad to see some other people are turned off by this woman as I am. If everyone in the world were as moralistically judgemental and perfect as Dr. Laura, I would hate to be here.

#17

I called Dr. Laura a few months ago to
discuss a conflict I was having with my husband
(who, incidentally is 15 years older than I
am). I never got to my question - she wigged
out and told me I was a girl with no history -
and that's what my husband gets for not
marrying a woman. I don't think that she ever
got past the fact that there was an age
difference.

Afterward, I began to notice that is her
method of madness. She doesn't have time to
discuss all the details, so she attacks the
first thing that doesn't fit into her black-
and-white view of the world. I've gotten over
my anger at being reduced to a Jerry Springer
guest on her show - but I've lost all respect
for her "advice."

#18
Why is anyone surprised by Dr. Laura's
behavior? She prides herself on her sarcastic
and abusive style. She has always approached
most problems on her show in this rude,
strident, insensitive manner which she peppers
with her sarcastic humor so it appears she's
making a good joke as she is skewering someone
calling in for help. The simmering rage that
is constant in Dr. Laura's voice comes through
clearly each day on her program.

When she speaks of little girls, her
disdain for them is palpable. She describes
how she is glad she had a boy and how little
girls are so much trouble. They are so vain,

cliquish, always talk about each other, are gossipy, and aren't good in groups. In fact, it's hard to find anything good she has to say about them. She has the same apparent opinion about women. It's quite frightening.

I listen regularly, not so much because I think she helps people, but because I find it facinating that people continue to call her. I occasionally even agree with her, but it's a sorry reflection of our world and how many people there are that choose to call a radio personality for instant abuse. They almost crave it.

If anyone criticizes her, her world becomes "The Caine Mutiny." All that's missing is the marbles. The journalist's hate her and has an agenda, she cries. Or they are "evil" or doing "evil." She detests liars, yet her husband lied that she was not being paid for her speech in Dallas, him justifying this lie because they hadn't actually received the check yet. Dr. Laura would ream a caller faster than you could blink if they tried to pull a stunt like that.

While she professes her "likes" as "people who take responsibility for their actions," and "dislikes" as "people who don't take responsibility for their actions," she refuses to take responsibility for her own rude, abusive behavior. Are having allergies an excuse for treating others badly? In Dr. Laura's world, I guess the answer is yes.

I wonder if, when her son is grown and is asked, "would you have rather been in day care or with your mother," Deryk will be one of the few who answers, "day care." Although it sounds like he is with his father more than his mother, which is a blessing.

Although I only hear her persona on her talk show, I concluded a long time ago that she is just not a nice person. This and all her other qualities make a successful, sensational talk show personality.

#19

I listen to Dr. Laura occasionally. I admire the consistent advice and value centered counseling approach she uses. However, I wonder how she arrives at her conclusions about her callers so quickly. She typically has only the most rudimentary information and background on the situations she advises upon. Isn't there an obvious danger in making such hasty judgements and issuing advisory opinions under these circimstances? Finally, I am surprised she continues to get plenty of callers. If there is any way Dr. Laura can turn the tables on the caller and get them to own the problem they are calling to complain about, she will. Rarely does these callers get much more than a pre-judged kick in the backside and a bit of blame to deal with as well. Just because she is a Dr., I find it hard to believe she can divine the full circumstances behind every caller's inquiry under such circumctances.

NOT ONLY IS DR. LAURA RUDE TO PEOPLE ON THE AIR, SHE IS ALSO RUDE TO PEOPLE SHE ENCOUNTERS IN HER PERSONAL LIFE.

#1

Dear Dr. Schlessinger:

A few weeks ago you recounted an irritating experience at a franchise ice cream shop. In the course of your monologue, unkind comments were made regarding the physical characteristics of the minimum wage teenage employee who had lied to you in front of his manager out of fear of losing his job. I would suggest that it is never appropriate to belittle an individual on the basis of their unchangeable physical traits, regardless as to how angry you might be over their actions.

#2

I thought Dr. Laura's remarks were COMPLETELY out of line when referring to a teenager in an ice cream parlor she visited. She talks about how much she loves children and then to disparage this young man on national radio for his physical appearance was completely remiss. She showed NO sensitivity to what could be a sensitive issue for him.

In addition, I wondered what kind of example this set for her son. Since she couldn't get her way regarding the ice cream cone, the rest of her family had to do without as well. Whatever happened to being flexible?

I wonder if the young man she criticized still has his job after her comments on the air about him. She prides herself in maintaining anonymity of characters in her story but she failed to do so in this instance. I'm sure people that frequent that shop could identify him based on her description.

I think she owes that young man a HUGH apology.

#3

It's always fun to get to see a celebrity up close and personal. That's why book signings and celebrity charity events are so popular. Sometimes it's a wonderful experience. Sometimes it dispels a lot of illusions. Last week was a perfect example in Dallas. Dr. Laura Schlessinger was here to speak at several cultural and fund-raising events. From the first, she was demanding. It has been much talked about that she refused the best suite at the Grand Kempinski Dallas hotel. But she also refused to stay in three others as well. She said the "smell" wasn't right. She finally accepted a suite at The Mansion on Turtle Creek, where she began making special food demands. One of her speeches was before the women's division of the Jewish Welfare Federation. Her hosts picked her up in a private car. She wasn't in the car for two minutes before she decided that this too "smelled." Someone had worn perfume. She then got out and hailed a cab. She went through three cabs before one smelled good enough to suit her.

She reportedly was not friendly at the donor reception and disappeared quickly, although her appearance was considered a part of her $30,000 speaker's fee. Her hosts gave her gifts, including Texas gifts for her young son. She left them all behind.

But the worst was how unpleasant and irritating she was in her speech. Before the evening was over, she had offended almost every woman in the room. There was barely any applause. Some people walked out. To the shock of many, Dr. Laura came off so abrasive and unpleasant that they weren't sure if even Ann Landers would know how to deal with her.

#4

Dr. Laura Schlessinger, who said she would return her speaker's fee to the Jewish Federation of Greater Dallas after a much-maligned appearance, has decided to do something else with the $30,000. Her personal assistant, Ernestia Osteen, said the syndicated radio talk show therapist has "changed her mind" about returning the money. "The money's still going to be given to a charitable organization, but it won't be the Jewish Federation," Ms Osteen said. Ms. Osteen said that Ms. Schlessinger "pretty much already had the charity in mind" that will receive the money.

#5

I travel frequently and talk to many airline employees who come in contact with Dr. Laura on her excursions to make appearances. As indicated in the Dallas visit, she acts just as you would expect her to.

I used to consider her talk show the "World Wrestling Federation" of Radio Psychology. You know, people get in the ring with her, get thrown around and she holds the belt over her head at the end of three hours. However, I have come in contact with some Professional wrestlers in my travels. My point is that these guys are pretty nice to people in airports and appearances, then put on a show when the bell rings. From what I have heard, Dr. Laura is a total Asshole on the radio and more so in real life. How bad do you have to be for your mother to not want anything to do with you?

Even Howard Stern is toned down if you are courteous to him. He doesn't go around touting "Moral Responsibility" either.

Listen to the show closely and ask yourself this. Laura Fans, would you really...really want to know this person in real life? Would you want this person as a friend? Would you? Knowing you would get a ration of #&^* by not tipping enough at a restaurant. Or for sending your kid to a certain school, or whatever choices you tend to make that she doesn't agree with. I think I would follow her mother right out the door.

CHAPTER FIVE
DR. LAURA ON THE OPRAH SHOW

Dr. Laura is a *hypocrite*. One of the things she stresses to people is to not associate themselves with people who are living dishonorable or unholy lives according to Dr. Laura's Law. Dr. Laura told a woman whose brother was having an affair and asked her to be Godmother to his baby with the other woman that she shouldn't bother with her brother again and that she should not bother with the child either. That is her brother and that child is her niece or nephew as much as the children with the wife are. In Dr. Laura's view, the woman should give up her brother for the rest of her life because he had a child with another woman. Pretty harsh I would say.

Dr. Laura also told a woman not to visit her son's home because he had his girlfriend living with him. Dr. Laura told the woman her son was immoral for living in sin and if she visited him she was also immoral. Dr. Laura, on the other hand, went on the Oprah Show to promote her new book. Oprah is living with a man she is not married to. In Dr. Laura's opinion that makes Oprah immoral. If Dr. Laura goes on Oprah's program, doesn't that make Dr. Laura (in her own words) immoral? After she did that I had to take action. I sent her this letter the day after her appearance on the Oprah Show. Of course I got no response from the good doctor.

Dr. Laura,
     I think you need to discuss "your"
morality here. I notice that you had no
problem being associated with a sinner that
furthers your financial cause, re: the
promotion of your new book. I also notice that
you never make "ANY" appearances until you have
something to promote. Very self-centered I
would say. A part of the "ME" generation. I
heard you tell a woman a few weeks ago not to
visit her son's home because he was "shacking
up" with a woman. What a hypocrite you are. I
see you had no problem visiting the Oprah show
even though she is "shacking up" with a man. I
guess since this involved putting money in your
pocket that makes it ok. I heard you comment
on all of the nice faxes you got about being on
the Oprah show. I marked the please comment
box on this fax but I'm sure that will never
happen, it doesn't make the "Good Dr." look
good.

     The reason Dr. Laura broke her own rules
of morality here is purely financial. She did
it only for the money. When I find letters like
this one, I have to insert it in the middle of
the paragraph. (start) I hate to admit it, but
early on I actually liked the "Dr.'s" show and
thought she was really giving good advice to
poor slobs who really needed it. But over time
I've come to realize that she is DEFINITELY in
it for the money; that there is NO subject she
won't render an opinion (usually a lousy one)
about and that pretty much nobody gets any help
from her. I have never heard her say, "I was
wrong about that." Dr. Laura does WAY more
damage than good with her arrogant, lousy,
opinionated sixty-second sound bites.

Dr. Laura reconsidered her morals because the cost of not being on the Oprah show (loss of revenue on her new book) was too high to assert it. This is capitalism at it's worst. If you take a look at Dr. Laura's Website, you will find that advertisers take up more than half of all of the pages on the site. Also on her Website she sells T-shirts, sweatshirts, hats, mugs, neckties, baby rompers, bibs and rattles, afghans, stuffed animals, license plate frames, keychains, computer screen savers, calenders, organizers, mouse pads, books, audio and video tapes. Advertisers on her radio program include ads for the day after pill and other euphemisms for abortion from a planned parenthood agency. There is also an ad with the narrator of the Motel 6 commercials focusing on a pregnant teenage girl keeping her baby. The girl gets up in the morning, feeds the baby, leaves the baby and goes to school, then she goes to work. The girl comes home at 10pm and feeds the baby, studies and goes to bed. The teenager gets up in the morning and the process starts all over again. The motto of the commercial – IT CAN BE DONE! These ads are played during Dr. Laura's program. These are actions the Dr. deems unacceptable. Why does she allow them to advertise on her show? MONEY!

Dr. Laura uses the pain and dysfunction of her callers for financial gain, which is unethical. Dr. Laura does not care about the quality of the lives of those that listen to or call her show. She is also not interested in helping them. She is concerned only with her self-advancement.

I received several letters about Dr. Laura's appearance on the Oprah Show on my web page and gathered more from other sources on the Internet.

#1

I saw Dr. Laura on Oprah Winfrey the other
day, plugging her new book, when something
occurred to me. Isn't it a bit hypocritical
for her to be advising people on her show not
to associate with people who do things that are
dishonorable and unholy, but then go on Oprah,
who is obviously "shacking up"?

#2

It was wrong for Dr. Laura to compromise
her beliefs. But, I do have to say that if Dr.
Laura did not interact with everybody who chose
a different life path, she would isolate
herself from a lot of people. Oprah has no
children and appears to try to be a good
person. Does everybody think that we should
disassociate from everyone who does something
that we don't agree with? I believe that
should depend on what that something is. I'm
not defending Dr. Laura, as I doubt that she
needs it. I'm just saying, again, as far as I
know, Stedman has his own home, Oprah has hers;
they probably do spend some nights together.
All I can say, I would not disassociate with
Oprah for this.

#3

I missed the second half of Dr. Laura on
the Oprah show. Did the subject of Oprah
"shacking up" ever come up? I guess the focus
was supposed to be on married couples, so that
made it comfortable for both Oprah and Dr.

Laura not having to address the fact of Oprah's living arrangements with Stedman over the past many years. Kind of ironic watching these young married couples making their way through their problems, trying to make things better, wanting to stay together and work things out…having Oprah for a guide, advisor, counselor, someone holding forth with all the right answers. Whatever….

#4

Do you share the same thought with me that Dr. Laura has put aside her values just to be able to advertise her book on Oprah!!! I mean she does not believe in shacking up (which Oprah does) and yet she closes her eyes on this point and goes on the Oprah show to discuss the Husbands Behaving Badly point of view ONLY!!! I mean wasn't that very obvious!!

I have not read her book yet, but I am sure that it does not only discuss the subject of husbands but also men in general in respect to their relationships with women. So please Dr. Laura, next time do not let money and advertising for your books blind you because if you do that, you will be like the rest of the people you condemn on your show!!!

Not discussing the subject of shacking up because Oprah is doing so is an unbelievable act for you!! I would have thought that this (the shacking up of Oprah) should have deterred you from doing the whole show!!! Didn't you say on one of your shows that if someone goes to an unwed mother's baby shower it is like saying, "I support what you are doing"? I do not think I have to say anything more.

#5

     I have lost a lot of respect for Oprah
over the past few years. She may have
wonderful audiences, but her values are
definitely skewed. For instance, a prominent
and well-known Baptist pastor from New Jersey
who is well known for his work with youth was
asked to speak on Oprah's show. However, prior
to his appearance, her people called back to
say that he was being axed from the list. Why?
Because he preaches abstinenance to youth!
Oprah's people told him that Oprah thought that
this was an impractical message to preach, as
kids were going to do it anyway, it was a
natural act, so you had best give them the
tools to keep it safe. Oprah and her staff are
full of today's change it as you go morality.
How Dr. Laura could look at Oprah with rose
colored lenses has baffled me.

#6
     If the idea is commerce, then it's o.k.
to be a hypocrite? I've listened to Dr. Laura
for a year, read her books and know without a
doubt that she encourages listeners not to
associate with people who follow a different
moral code. She is emphatically against
"shacking up." Whether her code or Oprah's
code regarding this is right is beside the
point. The fact that Laura preaches against it
time and time again, then has the audacity to
go on Oprah's show to peddle her wares is
spelled H-Y-P-O-C-R-I-S-Y.

#7

Whatever the given situation, be it Dr. Laura's or anyone else's…COMPROMISING ONES PRINCIPLES FOR MONETARY GAIN IS WRONG, WRONG, WRONG!!

#8

NOBODY forced Dr. Laura to appear on the Oprah show (whether she called the show of the show called her!!!) Financial reasons and trying to make a living is in no way a good reason to go against what you believe in, and I think the first person to agree with that point would be Dr. Laura. Oprah's shacking up is nobody's business, but Dr. Laura supported her by appearing on her show. Dr. Laura did not discuss the "shacking up" issue even though it appears in her book. Dr. Laura appeared on the Today show and the Late show to promote her book, and she promotes it everyday on her show, so financial disaster regarding the book was not a problem to her. The book was going to sell well anyway without having to compromise her values. My main problem with this whole thing is Dr. Laura's agreement not to discuss the subject of shacking up in return for her appearance on the show.

#9

I would venture to say that maybe Oprah does spend some nights with Stedman. From what I understood, she has her own home and he has his own home. Am I mistaken or misinformed?

Do we know for sure that Oprah is shacking up?
I missed the show with Dr. Laura. I know she
doesn't believe in people living together.
Maybe she doesn't knock people for what they do
unless they tell her or involve her in their
circumstances. I heard her say on her show
that she refrains from making comments to
people unless specifically asked. She also
said what she believes and how she feels but
that people have to make their own decisions
and their own choices.

#10
     I was so excited to see Dr. Laura on the
Oprah show. First, it is the Oprah show, but
with the power and authority that Dr. Laura
brings to the table, she was clearly renegated
to little more than a sniveling emotional feel-
good backdrop to validate Oprah's misguided
agenda for the topic. I appreciate that Dr.
Laura has feelings and shares them, but where
was the frank, spunky, in-your-face sensibility
to balance the feelings?

     The agenda was clearly to make men look
foolish, and buy into the surface appeal of
Laura's new book's title. I don't know why I
expected anything more than what I saw. Dr.
Laura's publicity people should be more
discerning with the appearances they arrange.
Each appearance should resoundly support the
credibility and candor that Dr. Laura posseses.

#11

I totally forgot that Oprah and Stedman are not married! This is not the first time Laura has been on Oprah either. I saw her a long time ago on the show giving relationship advice.

#12

Dr. Laura made a comment on the Oprah show that she and Oprah were "seperated at birth." I didn't see the show and I'm a fairly new Dr. Laura listener. Dr. Laura is extremely judgemental, but she seems mostly concerned with people being responsible. In other words, owning up to your actions, doing the right thing. Given Oprah has not had a baby out of wedlock and is also very outspoken when she feels someone is wrong or is misbehaving, I can see why Dr. Laura may have made this comment.

#13

Stedman and Oprah are not married and they are living together. Cut and dry. How can Dr. Laura say that she and Oprah were seperated at birth, when obviously they don't hold all the same values.

These letters are from fans that thought it was acceptable for Dr. Laura to compromise her principles - for whatever reason.

#1

Dr. Laura has a family to support.
Remember, her husband was laid off and then had
a bad heart problem and now stays home with the
kid. She works part time and makes enough to
see to it that her kid can go to private school
and college and that she and her husband will
be taken care of in their later years. Remember
that the average career span of a media
personality is very short and you have to
strike while the iron is hot. In five years
when her son is in high school if her show were
to be canceled, she may not want to work full
time and overtime to establish a new career.
I'm more disappointed in Dr. Laura fans that
watch Oprah.

#2

I would have liked to see more of the Dr.
Laura we know on Oprah's show. Dr. Laura said
that in her time there, they really
accomplished a lot. She said she had enough for
three shows and a LOT of editing went on.
Without being there it's hard to know what
really happened only how it was framed. She was
a GUEST on the show (it wasn't called Laura!).
I admit I prefer her telling it like it is
approach and tackling ethical dilemmas. But she
was working within the framework she agreed to,
and still managed to get across the idea that
prioritizing is what's important.

#3

Dr. Laura was definitely a background decoration for Oprah. Problem is that Oprah is really a second rate intellect who does shows full of cheap sentiment. Apparently Dr. Laura, who is light years smarter than Oprah, was a threat. Oprah was determined not to be upstaged by someone as brilliant as Dr. Laura. Hence, when the editing of the two or three hour show was boiled down to one hour, Dr. Laura was relegated to second place. In any worthwhile talk show, the guest is always the "star". Not the host.

#4

A good majority of people have a lot of respect for Oprah. Her show is high quality without the sleaze of the others in her profession. I'm sure Dr. Laura respects her as well. Let me ask you something: would you refuse to visit a good friend in HER home because her boyfriend lives there but they are not married? Why is it any business of yours what they do in their own home? They certainly don't have sex in front of you. Why should it be any of Dr. Laura's business if Oprah lives with Stedman? They aren't making any illegitimate babies. They both make a very good living and their reasons for NOT marrying are none of anyone's business. That is very PERSONAL. It would not be Dr. Laura's or anyone else's place to go on HER show (and be paid for being there) and insult the hostess or tell her you disapprove. She was on the show to promote her book and that's what she did.

#5

Dr. Laura went on the show because this is the real world, business. If Oprah called the Dr. Laura show unhappy or in a dilema, then she would have got an ear full. The fact is Oprah is o.k. with her life. The world is full of immoral people. Dr. Laura does business with the grocery guy whose shacking up!!!! OH NO! WHAT A SHAME the good Dr. isn't so good after all. Get off it, she doesn't care who does what UNTIL THEY ASK HER for her opinion.

Here are some faxes Dr. Laura received on this

controversial matter.

#1

I saw you on Oprah. Loved it. You did not ask her about her "shacking up" with Stedman. Why?

#2

I am curious to know how you felt doing the Oprah show knowing that she is co-habitating out of wedlock. Is it wrong to apply one's beliefs to other people's situations, like living together, when you disagree with their behavior or is that taking moral beliefs too far?

CHAPTER SIX

OFF THE AIR – OR SHOULD BE

As a result of Dr. Laura's rudeness and inconsistencies, she is being dropped off the airwaves of some radio stations. Some other listeners are requesting that she be dropped from their local stations.

Dr. Laura's show was bought by Jacor Communications, Inc. from Synergy Broadcasting, Inc in September, 1997. Jacor also acquired Multiverse Networks, LLC, the sales representation arm of the Dr. Laura show. Dr. Laura was added to Premiere Radio Networks, one of the country's leading syndicators of programming national talent to over 4,000 radio stations. Dr. Laura made this comment on the move:

"It's been tremendously rewarding to help make a difference to so many people. I am excited about the opportunities this acquisition presents to my show. We now will reach an even greater number of listeners."

Here are a few examples of Dr. Laura's show

being dropped off the air:

#1

Dr. Laura,
    I am really disappointed that our local
radio station has bumped you for another talk
show host they claim is more popular than you
are.

#2

    They have taken Dr. Laura off the air in
our town and replaced her with Dr. Joy Brown.
Dr. Laura is an advocate for parents raising
their own children. Dr. Joy Brown's only
advice is to tell stay at home moms to get a
job. If you listen to her you know what I
mean.

#3

    The Roanoke talk-news station has dropped
Dr. Laura. I don't blame the radio station for
their decision. They did what their ratings
book said to do. Certainly there are many
people in Roanoke who don't like having their
guilty consciences pricked by Dr. Laura. They
prefer to be soothed, stroked and coddled.

#4

    If you have been listening to the Dr.
Laura Schlessinger Show on Sunday's 9:00 to
12:00, you've noticed that it is being pre-
empted by the Sports Channel.

#5

Last month the Dr. Laura show as pulled
off the local Duluth station - both hours.
Totally. Permanently. They claimed that
afternoon ratings were very low. In place of
her show for the first hour they have a couple
of local guys talking about refrigerator
repair, computers, and insulation.

#6

Several weeks ago your program was taken
off our local radio station because of low, low
ratings.

#7

I was contacted by the Syndication
Company, which represents Dr. Laura's show. At
that time, we carried only the second and third
hours of her show, and they were calling to
DEMAND that we carry all three hours. I
informed them that, because the first hour of
Laura's show airs at the same time as the last
hour of Rush's show that we would NEVER carry
all three hours of her show.

They then DEMANDED that we record the
first hour of the show and play it back after
the live third hour, or play the extra five
hours on Saturday. I explained to them that we
do not carry ANY pre-recorded programming for
two reasons:

1. We're a small market station. We can't
afford to pay a producer to run the board for

two hours just to record and then replay one hour of her show, a show that has not produced any new advertising revenue for us. And...

2. We DO NOT run any delayed programming because: a) it's not fair to our listeners who want to call, and b) we can't afford it.

They then succumbed to "Limbaughitis." Limbaughitis is a syndrome which causes other nationally-syndicated talk show hosts or their syndicators to mistakenly believe that they could produce the listenership and advertising revenue for small-market stations that Rush Limbaugh has produced. Under the influence of this misperception they begin to attempt to use leverage which they simply do not possess. More directly, to use a phrase my father dearly loves, "They let alligator mouths overload their canary asses."

They gave me an ultimatum: Carry all three hours of the show, or we'll cancel your contract. I gave them a response: You can have two hours of your show on MY station, the ONLY station within 100 miles of the only metropolitan area in this quarter of the state, or nothing. They were shocked, "You can't give us an ultimatum, we're the syndicatior, WE give the ultimatums." But I can give them an ultimatum. I am the affiliate, the radio station, and the advocate for my listeners. I am the ONLY ONE who can give the ultimatums. My job is not to give the listeners what they need, as Laura believes she is doing. My job is to give them what they want, and they want Rush Limbaugh over Laura Schlessinger ANY DAY OF THE WEEK!

This is a lesson, which the syndicators of Laura's show had better learn: The affiliate radio stations which make up your network ALLOW your show to be on their stations. They were in business long before there ever was a "Doctor Laura Schlessinger Show," and they will still be in business long after both Laura and Rush have faded into obscurity.

Then we began to lose advertisers because of her comments and presentation. It was almost certain that her show would be canceled. For Laura's syndicators to ask us to drop an hour of Rush to carry the first hour of her show was actually kind of funny. I give them credit for being gutsy. But when Laura's syndicators had the audacity to DEMAND that we lose money by paying a producer to tape-delay her show, I stopped laughing. And I canceled the show.

I was giving Laura Schlessinger two hours a day on my station. It cost her nothing. I bought and maintained the equipment, I pay the electric bills, and I even had billboards printed promoting her show. She thanked me by kicking me in the teeth and saying, "You're not doing enough for me." Now, I truly know how her callers feel. - A Relieved Talk Radio Program Director of a FORMER Dr. Laura Affiliate Station

P. S. When the former program director replaced another talk show host with Laura, the station received by telephone, fax, and in person, 153 complaints in 2 days. Laura has now been off the air for two days, and we've gotten 4 (four) complaints… I think I'll go take on the day!

#8

As a marketing professional, I think you
have laid out sound reasons for not having Dr.
Laura's show on your station. I believe
callers are mercilessly ripped apart in order,
giving credit, to make a point, or being
cynical, to create radio drama and ratings. If
that is not the image of your station (it IS
the image of the station she is on in Los
Angeles) -- I support your removal action.

#9

Dear Dr. Laura,

My family moved from Charlottesville,
Virginia where I listened to your show to
Kingsport, Tennesee. Two days after our
arrival here one of the area's radio stations
announced on the air that they would be
cancelling your program. According to the
station manager you were a difficult person to
deal with. The following Monday the station
replaced your show with another Psychologist.

PLEASE TAKE HER OFF THE AIR!

Dear KRMG:

I have been a regular listener to your station for the past 25 years and have enjoyed your program format for the most part during that time. In recent years you have gone to more of a nationally syndicated format while featuring among others, Dr. Laura. I realize and appreciate the fact that these decisions are driven by market demands.

Unless I forget, or am not paying attention, I usually switch stations once Dr. Laura comes on. Occasionally I catch myself listening to her and some of the issues she espouses. I find two areas where she embraces outdated therapy that I have found can and does have fatal consequences. More specifically, issues dealing with childhood sexual abuse and alcohol/chemical dependency. If I understand her correctly, her methodology for dealing with these issues is:

1. Sexual abuse memories – put them in the past and get on with your life.

2. Alcohol and chemical dependency – get a little grit and assert your self-will.

Resorting to these methods of recovery is exactly what the usual sufferer instinctually attempts to do with dismal, and often-fatal results. This has been well documented to be a fatally flawed method of therapy.

In the case of sexual abuse memories, not confronting the memories and/or dealing with them in a therapeutic fashion often times results in transference of the abuse and/or suicide. Successful alcohol and drug professionals along with countless individuals who have recovered from the hopelessness of these diseases will tell you that the unaided use of "grit and self will" only tends to reinforce and progress the diseases, if the individual were a true alcoholic or addict.

I urge you to monitor this program and judge for yourself, and if you should find agreement with me, add my vote for you to make a community contribution and take her off the air before she contributes irreversible damage to one among us.

#2

Dear Dr. Schlessinger,
I know that you "don't do debates" and that this fax will probably end up in your round file. However, I feel compelled to send this after hearing a part of your show earlier this week.

I should let you know that I have voiced my displeasure to the program director of radio station CJAD in Montreal, for carryiing your show during the afternoon hours. As such, I have effectively boycotted the station after noon and often before that time. To me, a musician and a composer born and living in Canada, it is incredible that a program director in this country would import a syndicated show from the US, such as yours, during an important time slot. This is not your problem; but when combined with your reprehensible conduct on your show, it makes a regrettable situation worse.

In an afternoon earlier this week, when turning on the car radio I was subjected to your rant about "knocked up brides". Even though I am not in the habit of writing letters to the editor or calling radio stations in indignance, I promptly called the station to complain. The receptionist, bless her heart, claimed that the content of the show has nothing to do with CJAD. She did, however, give me your fax number. I was incensed that any health-care professional would use the term "knocked-up" at all, never mind repeatedly and in such a self-righteous rant. For me, it was the proverbial straw that broke the camel's back. I have heard you say on-air "knocked-up", "horny", "sluts", "screwing" and other charming terms a number of times and feel strongly that this is language unbefitting a professional therapist. I know this makes 'good radio' (just ask Howard Stern or Jerry Springer) but it makes me ill to hear this from a so-called professional psychologist. How do I explain these words to my 7-year-old who may be listening? I would respect no therapist who speaks in such a way, to say nothing of the moralistic, self-righteous, confrontational tone that is your trademark.

In closing, if you have read this far, or if you are reading this on the air in a mocking tone ala Rush Limbaugh, let me say that I have again voiced my opinion to the program director of the station. Furthermore, instead of grumbling in silence, I feel it is also important that you know how some people in this area feel about your tone and choice of language. That a number of your views are repugnant to me is irrelevant, radios come with on-off switches and channel changers, and I am free to use them when you are on. However, I feel whether I listen or not, the community standards that you so righteously strive to raise are being hurt by this kind of "shock talk".

PS: By the way, Larry Metzler does NOT orchestrate your music. The music on CD or record is already orchestrated; he perhaps chooses appropriate selections and co-ordinates them to fit in between commercial breaks. Orchestrating refers to the act of choosing specific musical instruments to play particular musical lines within a musical work. Orchestration is, indeed, a complex and technical musical endeavor, and has nothing to do with selecting CD's.

#3

I agree that Dr. Laura is on the right side of the religious right. I believe that Dr. Laura is so truly unchristian in her black and white opinions that she helps to make the religious right look even worse than they do on their own. I am a Christian. The beliefs I hold as a Christian are ones of love, acceptance, giving, and kindness. I nearly fell out of my chair the first time I heard Dr. Laura on the radio. She is extremely opinionated on issues she clearly knows nothing about. She is the most hateful, narrow-minded person I've heard in a very long time. Dr. Laura may have a degree in psychology, but somewhere along the way she forgot about the people a psychologist is supposed to help. What happened to the compassion and love for a person in pain? What happened to trying to understand where someone is in life and using your gifts, talents, or skills to help bring someone up?

I think Dr. Laura is far more harmful than any clinched-fisted fat preacher standing up before his congregation and preaching of the influences of the devil and hell. Many people don't hold in high regard anyone using religion as the basis for their arguments and because of that, much of the religious right is ignored. Dr. Laura on the other hand, uses the mystery and excitement of psychology to pull listeners into her web of hatred and narrow mindedness. I think she is doing every listener and this entire country a disservice. IF I CAN BE OF ANY ASSISTANCE IN EXPOSING HER OR GETTING HER OFF THE AIRWAYS, PLEASE INFORM ME AND I WILL BE HAPPY TO HELP.

CHAPTER SEVEN
ABORTION / ADOPTION

Dr. Laura's stand on abortion (or as Dr. Laura calls it "sucking it into a sink") is that it should never be done unless the mother's life is in grave danger from the pregnancy. Since she recently became Jewish, perhaps this belief came about because earliest Jewish law strictly forbade abortion as a way of avoiding childbirth, except when necessary to save the mother's life. She says this rarely happens, which is probably true. The fact is, abortion is a fact of our times.

Dr. Laura also blames abortion on the Women's Movement. The fact is, abortion has been practiced since the beginning of civilization. The Women's Movement urged that the decision to have an abortion be recognized under law as a fundamental individual freedom – a protected privacy right.

In Christian teachings, abortion was not proclaimed a sin until the end of the 1st Century A. D. Eastern and Western Catholic churches were split on the issue. The Eastern Church condemned abortion; the Western church condoned procedures during the early stages of pregnancy. Catholic doctrine today states that abortin is a mortal sin. Throughout the Middle Ages and the Renaissance in Europe, abortion was legal.

Abortion is a matter of personal choice. As long as abortion is a legal procedure in this country, no one has the right to judge a woman for having an abortion. No one has the right to decide for a woman what is right or wrong but the woman involved. Women have the right to control their bodies. Men have nothing to say about abortion, absolutely nothing. Men should really stay out of this issue. The only choice a man has when it comes to abortion is before the fact. If he doesn't want a woman to abort his child, he should keep his penis in his pants. That's a man's only choice. After the woman is pregnant, it's her choice whether to have the child or not. It's her body, it's her life, it's her choice, and it's the law. Obviously, on this subject I am pro-choice.

Abortion laws in the United States developed out of Anglo-Saxon tradition. For Centuries abortion prior to the movement of the fetus remained a private decision. The first restrictive abortion statute was passed in 1803. The nation's first court action on the issue was in 1812 in the Massachusetts Supreme Court. It ruled that abortion with the woman's consent was legal before fetal movement. The case was Commonwealth v. Bang. The most famous case, Roe v. Wade, in 1973 ruled that the privacy right encompassed a woman's decision to have an abortion. The Court held that states could not restrict abortions during the first trimester. Seventy-five percent of the world's population lives in nations where abortion is legal.

Perhaps no side of the abortion debate will ever change the thinking of the other

side. Neither side is willing to consent to
the possibility that the other side may be
right. That goes for both sides. Pro-lifers
won't consider that abortion might be the
perogative of the individual in the situation.
Perhaps it is just a clump of cells and the
soul doesn't enter the body until a later
point.

The Pro-Choicers won't consider the
possibility that it is not our decision who
gets to live and who does not.

Medical science has determined that a
fetus is not viable until it is at least 20
weeks old. Viability has to do with the
ability of the fetus to survive outside of the
womb.

Abortion is not for everyone but under the
current laws of our great country, women still
have abortion as an option to bringing a child
into the world that she doesn't want, can't
afford or is not equipt to properly care for.
I got a lot of response on this issue. Here
are some opinions on Dr. Laura's view of
abortion and adoption that I gathered in my
research.

#1

Dr. Laura,

On many of your shows you have stated your
opposition to abortion. I would like to make a
couple of points to you if I may:

> 1. Abortion is a private matter, one not
>   to be intruded upon by the government
>   or other individuals - what ever
>   happened to respect thy neighbor and
>   judge not, lest thee be judged?

What I am saying is that this decision is between a woman, hopefully the man, and her God, no one else.

The best way to prevent abortions is to provide sex education. It continues to confound me that several European countries have the lowest abortion rates because of the excellent sex education programs they provide to their youth. This country continues to be extremely uptight regarding sex education - especially parents that won't talk to their kids about sex and then bars the schools from educating them. Then we wonder why the teen birthrate and the abortion rate are so high.

#2

Your stand is commendable, however I was a victim of rape. Not acquaintance rape. I was attacked outside my apartment. As luck would have it, and to my horror I became pregnant. To me, there was only one decision - abortion. I would NOT bring a half-breed, scum kid into this world whose father perpetrated such a violent act. I hated the fact that I had to have this "thing" inside of me until I could get rid of it. I was GLAD, yes GLAD I did it and I was able to get on with my life. I now have a wonderful husband and a normal life. He knows about what happened and knows I made the right decision. I am now older and wiser and a lot stronger. If I was EVER in that situation again, I would beat the crap out of him and believe me he would wish he never saw me. While I respect your position, until you have had the experience, you can't begin to understand.

#3

   I don't understand why people who don't
have to go through something as painful as
having a child and trying to decide not what is
only good for the child but what is good for
them. I'm pro-choice, even though I never
thought that I would be, but you have to put
yourself in the other person's shoes. Such as,
what if they are young, unmarried and have no
way of supporting the child. They are scared
and they don't know what to do. At this point
emotions are running high. They do what they
have to do to do survive. Though I am pro-
choice I however don't think that people who
are living a high-risk life and have gotten
pregnant before should keep having abortions.
But there are cases where I think having an
abortion is the right way to go for that
person.

#4
   How would you feel when your child got old
enough and went looking for you and you had to
explain things to them and deal with all that
resentment? Not to mention explain that the
reason you aren't with his or her father is
because even though he said that he loved you
and talked about marriage he decided not to at
the last minute and decided to go with someone
else. Dr. Laura shouldn't jump to conclusions
about things until she knows all the facts.

#5

Let me say first that I do to not agree with abortion in many instances. I have never had an abortion and hopefully never will be put in a position to do so.

Many of us like to make the statement - abortion is murder and no one for any reason should ever have one. It is a private issue and no one should ever for any reason interfere.

#6

Pro-Choice does not mean Pro-Abortion. No one is FOR abortion. We all know and can prove when physical life begins. Only God knows when it has a soul. The fact is that no one knows if abortion is the death of a human being.

#7

Good for the mother who called you whose daughter was raped for forcing her to have an abortion. I'm glad she had the sense to get rid of the scum inside her daughter. I don't consider a glob of tissue to be a baby. A baby isn't a baby for several months. How DARE you tell a rape or incest victim that she HAS to carry the "thing" to term? It's her body, not the body of the rapist.

#8

Please don't label people who are for an individual's right to decide for themselves on this Pro-Abortionist! I HATE the idea of abortion but I think that my wife and I have the right to decide what we will do if we ever have to face such a terrible decision. Pro-Abortion sounds like we love abortions and that we are actively promoting the slaughter of unborn children. Believe me - WE ARE NOT! This is why the radical religious right 'Pro Lifers' often uses this term. They might as well call us 'Pro-Death'. These terms are used to inflame emotions and demonize people with opposing viewpoints. Please call us 'Pro Choice'.

There are a lot of gray areas on this issue. That is why I am for the right of individuals to choose on this issue. We know when life physically begins, but only God knows when it acquires a soul. As simple-minded humans, we can only "GUESS!" at what God knows.

Obviously the Supreme Court of the United States agrees.

Here are some views on adoption:

#1
True, there are a lot of adoption ads. 99% of them want "HEALTHY WHITE NEWBORNS". What about children with handicaps? What about OLDER children? There are a lot of "throwaways", abused and neglected children that need parents. Why do people only want healthy WHITE infants? For the same reason everyone wants a puppy or kitten. When they get older they aren't "cute" anymore.

#2

I had an abortion. Adoption was never an
issue for me. I wouldn't want anyone else
raising my child. I made a mistake, however, I
shouldn't be condemned for it. I did what was
right for me and I don't regret it. I wasn't
ready for a child. I don't know how I would
feel every time I walked down the street and
saw a child that was around the age my child
would be and wonder if it was mine. Adoption
wasn't for me. I did what I had to do to
survive and if you condemn me for that you are
no better than me.

#3

There is no shortage of kids ALREADY HERE
who may not be available for adoption, but who
desperately need safety, food, clothing, and
medical care. A conservative said that the
world population will level off in 50 years and
that we will still have enough food. Even if
the population does slow down, it will be
because of the birth control fanatics, not
despite them. I'd love to see how Dr. Laura
would analyze the issue of morals versus the
law.

CHAPTER EIGHT

LIVING TOGETHER / PREMARITAL SEX

In Dr. Laura's world no one should be living together unless they are married. Let me remind you again that Dr. Laura has herself lived with a man without the benefit of marriage. Who is she to judge what other people do, especially when she has already done the same thing? It is no one's business if two adults opt to live together. There are many reasons people decide not to get married. Some people just don't want to be married, period. Some who have been married before, don't want to marry again. Some don't get married for financial reasons. Does that mean that you can't be with someone you love on a permanent basis?

Dr. Laura says that by moving in together people are avoiding life and the struggles that come with it. When two people live together, there are the same problems that there are in a marriage. There are jobs, working on the relationship, household chores to do, yardwork to be done, bills to pay and if there are children, they still have to be raised. What are they avoiding? Life goes on as usual. There is just not a piece of paper joining you by law.

Marriage has nothing to do with religion. If that were the case, you could go back to the same church you got married in to dissolve the marriage if it doesn't work out. You would not need a LAWYER. You would not have to spend money paying two (one for each of you) lawyers. You don't need a piece of paper to be joined by the heart.

Dr. Laura also states that you cannot have a committed relationship unless you are married. The definition of commitment is "The state of being bound emotionally or intellectually to someone or some course of action." It does not say 'marriage license' in the definition. A marriage license doesn't make you feel any more love for a person.

In my research I came across some Census Bureau facts. In 1960 there were 439,000 couples living together, 197,000 with children under the age of 15. In 1995, there were 3,668,000 couples that lived together, 1,319,000 with children under the age of 15. Also, the fact on single parenting is that in 1968 there were 8,332,000 single parent homes. In 1995 there were 18,938,000 single parent families, 5,862,000 of who were never married mothers. Obviously, the trend is changing. There is NO longer a stigma to living together, or unmarried women having children, as there should not be.

#1 "Shacking Up"

This came from Dr. Laura's on-line column: Question: My boyfriend and I have decided to move in together. We have discussed our future and plan to be engaged in the next couple of months and to be married, perhaps next summer. My parents are not happy that we will be living

together before our engagement. They have
distanced themselves from my boyfriend and me,
and I am very hurt. I am hurt that they will
not accept my decision. I am in my late 20's
and am an adult! How do I deal with this?
Answer: (from Dr. Laura) YOU are hurt. How do
you think your parents feel? They did all the
work in establishing a home with commitment and
values, and they have to accept your decision
to disrespect all they have lived for and lived
up to? I'm sure they are aware of your age.
Since when does someone's age earn the person
acceptance and respect? It is by their actions
that the appropriateness of the respect is
decided. You made a choice to reject the values
of posponed gratification and the sanctity of
sex and co-habitation within a commitment – and
in doing so, you have disappointed and shamed
your parents. YOU made that choice. An adult
(which you are so anxious to indicate you are)
accepts the consequences of their choices.

This response if from the question/answer
section above.

#1
      I recently read Dr. Laura's answer in the
online to late 20's question. (How to deal with
parents on her living with boyfriend). Not a
good answer, Dr. Laura. The parents do not have
to accept their daughter's decision. They can
tell her they don't like it but to distance
themselves from her because she thinks
differently. All I can see here is "If you
think differently from me you are not
acceptable." This is groundwork for the biggest
injustice. Discrimination. Think with your head
not your emotions, Dr. Laura. Commitment is
inside the individual, not on a piece of paper.

Other "Shack-Up" Responses

#2

Dr. Laura,
      You frown about common law marriages, but
what if you are not religious? Is our love not
recognized by anyone but us? Does this mean we
are not considered decent people or is our
morality questioned because we don't believe in
a kindly grey haired old guy?

#3
      Dr. Laura frequently says shacking up is
immoral. Why? Because God says? If so, where?
If not, then is the fact that it undermines
society's building blocks enough for it to be
considered immoral? Even if no kids are
involved? Is there a more compelling reason? Is
there a moral distinction between premarital
sex, shacking up, shacking up with kids? If it
is not a moral issue, then what kind is it (a
motorcycle helmet kind)? Why should it be
discouraged? Should it be? On what grounds can
it be discouraged?

#4
      I define immoral as evil. I do not believe
shacking up or premarital sex is evil. If two
consenting adults have premarital sex before
marriage or want to shack up, I do not consider
it immoral. From a religious point of view, I
define it as unholy. As a standard for our
society, less than ideal. The ideal is
monogamous heterosexual marital sex. I do not
believe that committing either of these two

115

acts characterizes a person as immoral. I don't
put it up there with murder or rape or maiming
or adultery. I understand Christians consider
these issues grievous sins. I respect that.
That's your belief. I take a more moderate
stand on these issues. As to my personal
judgement, I probably agree with every reason
anyone has ever given for it not to take place
except immoral, but I cannot believe God will
judge us if we partake in either of these two
deeds.

I am not even sure if Dr. Laura's stastics
were correct that the divorce rate is higher
among couples who shack up. I know couples who
have shacked up. Some of them have divorced and
others are sticking with it. As to premarital
sex, I see nothing wrong in doing anything you
want sexually if you so desire.

#5
Defining morality in terms of good and
evil makes sense. The bible is chock-full of
commandments that most people do not follow. As
long as the actions of two consenting adults do
not bring about evil, they are not acting
immorally. The Ten Commandments (which contain
a bulk of the moral law) do not mention
premarital sex or shacking up. I see the
situation as less than ideal but not immoral.
As for children living with shack ups, it may
be unfair to the children, it is less than
ideal, but again it is not immoral. As for
premarital sex and shacking up being immoral
because it changes society – divorce changes
society far worse, and that is not immoral.

#6

Dr. Laura, as far as I know (I've been listening to her for a few months), has never said that anyone, no matter who they are, is right when living together without the benefit of marriage. But that one fact of 'shacking up' doesn't nullify all of the rest of the good in that person and she knows it.

#7

I've tried to call in to Dr. Laura, but I never can get through. I'm a gay male, and I've been committed to another man for the past two years. We live together. We're committed to each other for the rest of our lives. Because we can't get married, are we 'shacking up'? Is my situation "different" or am I being immoral because I live with someone whom I can't marry (legally)?

#8

I find Dr. Laura a real pain with her unrealistic views and preaching. From the crowing about "shacking-up" to how people under 20 are immature and unable to make adult decisions, I've heard just about enough from this California nut. Just because two adults share a household, her assumptions are that they are indulging in some illicit sexual conduct…perhaps this is the only way they can afford to live in a comfortable manner, by sharing expenses and not necessarily beds.

Not everyone can afford to live south of the boulevard Dr. Laura. And I suppose that two men or two women sharing a dwelling is OK with Dr. Laura… but what if they are Homosexuals or Lesbians… a point I'm sure she overlooked. As far as young adults not being mature at 18 and 20, she should remember that these immature "kids" are protecting this country by serving in the military, but for that I'm sure she'll say "that's different". Also most of the elderly who are now celebrating their 50, 60, and yes 70 years of wedded bliss were married in their late teens or early 20's… contrary to Dr. Laura's narrow views of immaturity and responsibility. I am having difficulty determining who has the more grating personality… Dr. Laura Schlessinger or the other blowhard… Rush Limbaugh. Notice how Dr. Laura doesn't have E-mail. I guess she can't stand criticism.

#9

I fully support Dr. Laura's stand on premarital sex. It is the ideal situation to find the "right" person, get married, and have sex on the wedding night. However, what if you don't want to get married? I have been married, had a nasty divorce, currently a single parent, like sex, and never want to remarry. The question is, for determined bachelors or those who have been burned by divorce, should they forfeit their sex life forever?

#10

Sex when two people love each other is the best kind of sex there is. However, sexual desire is a biological thing that humans have attached emotions to. While I'm not advocating jumping in the sack with every Tom, Dick, and Harry, sometimes people feel the need to be sexual with someone they don't necessarily love. They may care about the person, but it's sex for the sake of sex, with no emotional attachment. If two consenting adults have sex using protection, with an understanding of the nature of the relationship and having agreed on the reasons for having sex, why is that sad, to you? If you truly love someone, nothing can cheapen the joy of having sex with them. Sexual experience is a good thing. I personally would not marry a man I had not slept with. Good sex is such a joy in life that I think it's an important thing to find out what kind of lover a person is, and if you are compatible with him in bed before you commit the rest of your life to him.

CHAPTER NINE

HER KID'S MOM ???

Dr. Laura's opening statement on her show every day is "And Me, I Am My Kid's Mom." I have always wondered what she means by that. I am my childrens mother and so are all of the other mothers in the world. She makes a point of separating mothers into catagories: stepmother, adopted mother, foster mother, etc. To me we are all mothers. This little excerpt came from an internet site. - The first time I heard Dr. Laura's show I heard the opening line "And ME, I am my kid's mom". The second time I tuned in, once again I heard her give the opening credits at the top of the hour, "And ME, I am my kid's mom". Well, that was all just adorable, except that I'd heard her announce that she was her kid's mom the day before, so I figured the station was accidentally replaying yesterday's episode. I started listening to Dr. Laura from time to time and began finally to understand that she said she was her kid's mom *every damned hour on the hour.* Dr. Laura was hired to host a 3-hour national radio show five days a week because *SHE* is her *kid's freakin' mom.*

Dr. Laura's son Deryk burned down the house when he was 6-years-old. The next year he spray painted his room. Was she being "Her kid's mom" when these things were happening? Where was that 24 hour surveillance she is always talking about children should have when this was transpiring?

Here are some letters from others who are dumbfounded by the statement "And ME, I am my kid's mom".

#1
    What does it mean to be "your kid's mom?" Why can't a Dad be a "kid's dad." One of your shows had a Dad say that he told Caroline that he was his "kid's Dad." He left the impression that Caroline said he could not be. There was no further comment from you on this issue.

#2
    I've listened to Dr. Laura's show on and off for about a year. What bothers me is her intolerance toward divorce. If you are a woman who's married a divorced man with kids, you're a jezebel in the eyes of Dr. Laura. Even if the second wife has had nothing to do with the husband's divorce. Dr. Laura condemns her for "marrying a man with a past." The second wife is supposed to come last on the totem pole of the new husband's priorities - behind his first wife and children, even if the children live with the first wife and not in the home of the father. She is so intolerant of second marriages that it makes one wonder about her own past.
    Her attitude toward working mothers is so completely hypocritical it makes my blood boil. She works! She makes about $5 million a year! Yet she trumpets the "My Kid's Mom" thing as though the little aphorism made any sense at all.

#3

Dr. Laura,
    I heard you and a caller talking about
wrestling with your children. As a mother of
three, I never wrestled with any of them. I
played with them, gave them lots of affection
but I never, ever wrestled with them. I knew
if I did that at some point they would be
stronger than I would and there would be a
physical standoff of some kind. I think there
is a line you do not cross as a parent and one
of the things on the other side of the line is
wrestling.

#4

    More recently Dr. Laura has had little
Deryk giving us advice. His life experience
plus the fact that he is his mother's son
definitely qualifies him as a psychotherapist
also. What I would like to see is what Ms.
Laura (I don't like to call her doctor) will do
when little Deryk becomes a teenager and the
hormones kick in. How is the perfect mother
going to reconcile her beliefs in late marriage
and virginity until marriage. And how she would
convince horny Deryk to wait until he is
thirty, properly married, with a doctoral
degree and a talk show of his own, before he
will be allowed to have intercourse. She would
probably cut his allowance and of course, never
speak with him again. How idiotic.
    I pity her callers because they are
dysfunctional people, who obviously know no
better, or like to be abused. I pity her son
and husband even more because they have to live
with her every day. As for her black belt in
Karate, when was the last time she proved her

fighting skills in a real fight? These days, black belts come a dime a dozen, real fighters come less often. Talk show hosts come a dime a dozen, real therapist less often.

#5
I wish I could ask Dr. Laura the following questions:
1. Who raised her kid while she was getting her Ph.D.? And who is raising him while she is pursuing her radio talk show career and possibly a therapy practice?
2. Why does she never mention her husband? Does she indeed have one?
3. How can she presume to judge other peoples' lives (but then that begs the question, how can people be so stupid as to let her?)
Dr. Laura tells people not to go to a sperm bank to have a child. The child will find out that the husband is not his/her father and the child will be devastated. Dr. Laura went to a sperm bank to have Deryk because her husbands sperm count was low. Her statement was "They mixed his sperm with the donors so it's a possibility that Deryk is his child. He looks like a miniature version of me anyway, so it doesn't matter." If her husband couldn't make a baby with his sperm alone, how could Deryk be his child?

AND THE REAL QUESTION IS, "*WHO IS HER KID'S DAD*"?

CHAPTER TEN

DR. LAURA'S BOOK REVIEWS

Ten Stupid Things Women Do To Mess Up Their

Lives

#1
     Laura Schlessinger skewers her own sex in this surprisingly dull tome. Painting all women with the same broad brush, she presumes to inform females of their multiple failings. Fans of her show will love this book.

#2
     My boyfriend recently received a copy of Dr. Schlessinger's book "The Ten Stupid Things Women Do To Mess Up Their Lives." Much to my dismay, after reading the book he reported to me that he believes that it is a woman's fault if she finds herself in a violent domestic relationship. I don't think that Dr. Schlessinger has thought the situation of domestic violence through very well, or she wouldn't have such trite solutions to offer. Thankfully, I was available to bring these issues up for my friend's consideration, which enabled him to completely reevaluate his previous stance on the subject, but I worry now about how many people are not prepared to combat this type of ignorance.

#3

Your book, Ten Stupid Things Women Do To Mess Up Their Lives, is nothing but a list of obvious comments and insensitive remarks. Abused women don't stay with their abusers because they are stupid nor because they like it, they have low self-esteem and have never learned that they deserve better. Your comment on women living with a man before marriage is your opinion, that stems from your own insecurity and need to play power games.

Ten Stupid Things Men Do To Mess up Their Lives

In ten chapters, Dr. Laura gives her opinion on:

Stupid Chivalry - By getting involved with the wrong woman you think that your love can save/transform her.

Stupid Independence - Unwilling to admit "need" for bonding and intimacy, you hide in excesses of work, play, drink, drugs, porn, and meaningless sex.

Stupid Ambition - Unable to comfortably and proudly accept your inherent importance to society and family as husband and father, you bow to the false idols of money, toys, power, and status.

Stupid Strength - Uncomfortable with feeling weak, vulnerable, useless, powerless, or rejected, you use intimidation, force, or passive - aggressiveness to regain control.

Stupid Sex – Taking an attraction, opportunity, or erection as a "sign," you measure your masculinity and power by sexual conquests, infidelities, and orgasms.

Stupid Matrimony – Lacking a mature sense of the purpose, meaning, or value of marriage, you realize too late you've gone down the aisle with the wrong woman for the wrong reasons and feel helpless to "fix it."

Stupid Husbanding – Thinking that marriage is the honorable discharge from loving courtship, you continue to live as though you were single and your "mommy-wife" will take care of everything else.

Stupid Parenting – Believing that only women/mothers nurture children, you withdraw from hands-on parenting to assert your masculine importance, missing out on the true "soul food" of a child's hug.

Stupid Boyishness – Having not yet worked out a comfortable emotional and social understanding with your mother, you form relationships with women that become geared to avenge, resolve, or protect you from your ties to Mommy.

#1

This book is guilty of some uncharacteristically fuzzy thinking, which allows Dr. Laura to vent against some of her favorite foes – that monolithic block of fanatics known as "The Feminist" (who are a bitter, undifferentiated, and irrational crew,

126

in Schlessinger's opinion), and to excuse men, to some degree, from their irresponsible and self defeating behavior. According to Schlessinger, one of the main causes of male irresponsibility in contemporary society is gender role confusion caused by a culture dominated by "feminism," which she seems to equate with a very rigid style of liberal feminism that denies all psychological and biological differences between men and women, and which is fundamentally anti-male. As a feminist who has taught Women's Studies (another one of Dr. Laura's nemeses), I can vouch authoritatively for the fact that feminism is a much more complex phenomenon than this, and by no means unformly, or predominately anti-male. By blaming "The Feminist" (equated with culture) Schlessinger manages, to some degree, to let men "off the hook" for their reprehensible behavior. Although Schlessinger never allows women that same latitude, (feminist claims that women have been oppressed by centuries of male dominated culture – as evidenced by mere historical details such as women's deprivation of legal and civil rights relative to men's over the centuries – are, according to Dr. Laura, illegitimate and irrelevant in explaining women's self defeating behaviors).

Dr. Laura's aggressively pro-male stance, ironically enough, leads the reader (at least the female reader) to a sense of despair over "mankind". Her chapter on "Stupid Husbanding'" for example, presents such a lengthy litany of male irresponsibility, insensitivity, and just plain stupidity that any sane woman would run screaming rather than commit to a relationship with a member of a sex so clearly unsuited to matrimony. Moreover, her biological determinism – maleness is an "animal" trait, which must be overcome, but being a man is "human," and to be striven towards – is rather insulting to men. Male biology somehow makes men less than human, and huge amounts of effort must be exerted in order for them to achieve human connection and civilized behavior.

#2 A prima donna mentality.

In this particular book, Dr. Laura wants to argue both sides of the fence. On one hand, many behaviors assumed masculine are stupid, but she wants men to be masculine when she wants her doors held open, her meals paid for, etc. I think it was in the "stupid marriage" chapter where she tells men to avoid 'androgynous' women. Now what basis does she use for saying that there should be masculinity, and femininity? The Torah? Supernatural signs and wonders? No! Her own opinion! Presented as Divine Law, equal to the Ten Commandments. It's an attitude of arrogance, that women think they have a right to dictate masculinity, any more than when men used to dictate femininity to women. Instead of the subservient woman, we have a new kind of anti-feminist: the woman who can do whatever she wants, but HE has to pay for my meals.

#3 Primal Man Rules

I had the gut wrenching experience of skimming this book. I am healthy, good looking, successful, driven, intelligent and have attained a higher consciousness when it comes to viewing life from the street-vs-10,000 feet.

Subsequently I have had the proper introspect when it comes to what being a man is all about. In an infinite world it is purely subjective. Unless you view things from a strict Catholic/social/female centered perspective, which Dr. Laura does. Of course from a woman's perspective a man is messing up his life when he wants to do it "my way". Because that is the way of primal man - multiple partners, independence, variety, and embracing his inner child.

Those of us who are strong enough to maintain this individual solidarity won't be walking schmucks in shopping malls with the Dr. Laura's of the world ear beating us with such inane text.

#4 Dr. Laura's Cookie Cutter World

Like many talk radio listeners, I was drawn in by Dr. Laura Schlessinger's refreshingly frank approach to marriage and family therapy. How nice that someone had the courage to stand up to the increasingly victim-centered world in which we live. If Dr. Laura's philosophy stopped there, she would be a national treasure. Instead, on her show and in the book, she reveals herself instead to be a typical right wing anti-feminist, content to reap the benefits of the changing world without acknowledging how much of her career is possible only because of the work of some feminist she claims to disagree with. Schlessinger claims to be pro-child but her true nature is not pro-child but anti-woman. How else to explain the ridiculous assertion (made on the show) that working motherhood is "always a choice". This may be true for the

privileged world of radio personalities,
college professors and family therapists, but
for many others, working is the difference
between living on the street and keeping the
family alive. Stereotyping working women as
materialistic and self-centered is evil. It
would be easy to write-off Schlessinger as a
typical woman-hater, but the truth as revealed
in this book shows that her perspective on men
isn't much broader. I read the book without
recognizing behavior of any of the many men in
my life. In Schlessinger's world, all men like
sports and all women like to shop. She has no
understanding of the true diversity of life
that makes the world so fascinating and
priceless. How sad that people think of this
silly woman as wise. She is as narrow-minded
as they come.

#5

     Dr. Laura does not bash men; however, her
new book "Ten Stupid Things Men Do To Mess Up
Their Lives" most certainly does. On page 38
she states "a man is measured by his ability to
fight." Not his brain, not his heart, not his
maturity, his sense of humor, etc. Simply by
his strength and aggression. Furthermore, Dr.
Laura thinks this is a good thing, and calls
any male who doesn't excel in these qualities
'self-emasculated'. I find it hard to reconcile
this attitude toward men on her show. Perhaps
her book was ghost written!

#6

I made it through a chapter and a half of
Dr. Laura's latest book, one of the "Ten Stupid
Books That Mess Up People's Lives." I can't
believe that I paid hardcover price for a book
I can't read past page thirty-eight. Dr. Laura
wastes no time getting to the question of why
'nice guys' can't attract women. On page eight
she gives three reasons why 'nice guys' are
UNWORTHY of love. 'Nice guys' in her view are
either wolves in sheeps clothing, eunuchs in
the harem or looking for love in all the wrong
places. In each case the problem comes down to
a lack of AGGRESSION.

She makes this even more abundantly clear
on page thirty-eight, where she says 'The
AGRRESSIVE, STRONG, DETERMINED, POWERFUL,
HIGHLY SEXUAL MALE is the biological match for
the female. The human animal 'nice guy' having
chosen to divest themselves of maleness, don't
attract women as mates – just as best friends.

Of all the traits that make up my
personality, I do not find aggression to be
strong among them. Oh, I'm competitive enough,
but it's an intellectual sort of competition. I
prefer to build myself up rather than knock
someone down. I consider aggression to be the
root of evil, pure and simple. Nine out of the
ten commandments are against forms of
aggression. The sole exception is number two,
against bowing down to false idols.

Until I read that paragraph I never
equated aggression with attractiveness to
women. My other single 'nice guy' friends are
as non-aggressive as myself. Lacking even the
simpliest aggressive tendencies, I am truly
fishing without bait.

#7

I have a real problem with defining caring
as 'feminine' and aggression as 'masculine'. I
will agree that, in general, men are less
caring and more aggressive than women, and that
it comes from the biology, not just from the
culture. However, I know a lot of guys who do
not fit this pattern. Good guys. Moral guys.
Caring guys. Hard working guys. VERY LONELY
GUYS. Why? If I am to believe Dr. Laura, it's
because women don't think of these guys as MEN.

Read what Dr. Laura has to say about 'nice
guys' in her latest book, "Ten Stupid Things
Men Do To Mess Up Their Lives." It is hateful.
She says that a woman isn't attracted to a nice
guy, that she shouldn't be, and that if she
somehow ends up with one, she will either leave
him or make his life miserable.

My real point is that Dr. Laura believes
that there is only one sort of woman or one
kind of man to be. Anybody who is outside of
this narrow definition is 'self-emasculated' or
'dysfunctional'. I don't believe in perfect,
cookie-cutter people and I don't want to be
one. I feel the stress every day from those who
are trying to make me something I'm not.

#8 Just as bad as the book about women.

Dr. Laura should have grown up in my
family. My mother is the sports fan and my
father loves the soaps. They both worked and we
grew up as very happy "latch key" children. In
this book Dr. Laura (the physiologist)
attempts, in her tedious prose, to
compartmentalize men as she did women in her
previous book. She is more lenient with the

guys however, blaming a lot of their "stupid" activities on their women. A well-known hater of her own sex, Schlessinger seems to be using her books for the sole purpose of attacking women.

How Could You Do That?

#1

Laura talks better than she writes. The best parts of this book are the transcripts from the radio show. Why? Her writing hits the page with a thud. There's simply no life in it.

Her topic is an interesting one, but this book does not succeed in making it's point. I would be hard-put to find a reader who enjoyed the book who doesn't already listen to her show AND was a rabid fan. I'm not discussing whether or not I agree with her position, but how she communicated it.

#2

In print, as in her national radio show, Dr. Laura Schlessinger comes across as an improbable mixture of Joan Rivers and Marilyn Quayle. She is abrasive, smug, and a little too sure that her way is the only way. Her pro-child stance is ridiculously overblown and her well documented dislike of women is a disturbing reflection of a world that, while ready to give women equal rights, is just as ready to blame them for the break down of the family. I've read all three of Schlessinger's books, in part to try and understand the rabid following that hangs on her every word, and it appears that Schlessinger belongs to the group of thinkers that wax nostalgically for the perfect world of a past that never was. Schlessinger blames the state of the world on a decline in values, while ignoring the racism and sexism that fueled the world prior to this shift. Her lack of compassion for those who are born into circumstances less privileged than her own is disturbing to say the least.

#3

The book was common sense and OK. Have you heard her talk show? I used to like her but don't care to listen to her anymore. There is no need to be rude or put a caller down. There are better ways of handling things and she does not do well!! Some of her values are fine yet others I do not agree with. She acts as if she is perfect and I am sure she has made several mistakes in her life. She is a waste of airtime.

#4

I think we all wish for someone in our lives who has all the answers, especially simple ones that can be summarized into little lists or slogans. Life is much more complicated and muddled than that, however, and I am always cautious to hear or read anything that smacks of too much "certainty". The idea that there is "one way" to think about an issue (especially when it comes to placing blame or responsibility for a problem) just runs counter to my own thinking about how people get

themselves and others into difficulty.
Certainly there is such a concept as
responsibility, and sometimes we'd like to
shirk it. However, sometimes people do
seemingly "dumb" things for reasons OTHER than
simply wanting to take the easy way out. This
lady just seems in my view, to be getting off
on being a domineering mom. A little empathy
might bring her closer to understanding why and
how people screw up and to realize that there
are ways to resolve problems without pointing
such punitive fingers at people.

TEN COMMANDMENTS – THE SIGNIFICANCE OF GOD'S
LAWS IN EVERYDAY LIFE (as if Dr. Laura knows
anything about everyday life)
(Jerusalem Bible, Korean Publishers, Jerusalem)

Dr. Laura Schlessinger and Rabbi Stewart Vogel
are working on a book about the Ten
Commandments. Especially if you are Christian
Clergy we would appreciate you answering the
following 18 questions at whatever length you
desire. Please indicate your religious
affiliation and/or "ordination." Thank you for
your help!
1. I am the LORD thy GOD, who have brought thee
out of the land of Mizrayim, out of the house
of bondage.
2. Thou shalt have no other Gods besides me.
Thou shalt not make for thyself any carved
idol, or any likeness of anything that is in
heaven above, or that is in the earth beneath,
or that is in the water under the earth: thou
shalt not bow down to them, nor serve them: for
I the LORD thy GOD am a jealous GOD, punishing
the inquiry of the fathers upon the children

unto the third and fourth generations of those
that hate me; but showing mercy to thousands of
generations of those that love me, and keep my
commandments.

3. Thou shalt not take the name of the LORD thy
GOD in vain; for the LORD thy God will not hold
him guiltless that takes his name in vain.
4. Remember the Sabbath day, to keep it holy.
Six days shalt thou labor, and do all thy work:
but the seventh day is the Sabbath to the LORD
thy GOD: in it thou shalt not do any work,
thou, nor thou son, nor thy daughter, thy
manservant, nor thy maidservant, nor thy
cattle, nor thy stranger that is within thy
gates: for in six days the LORD made heaven and
earth, the sea, and all that is in them, and
rested on the seventh day: therefore, the LORD
blessed the Sabbath day and hallowed it.
5. Honor thy father and thy mother: that thy
days may be long in the land which the LORD thy
GOD gives thee.
6. Thou shalt not murder.
7. Thou shalt not commit adultery.
8. Thou shalt not steal.
9. Thou shalt not bear false witness against
thy neighbor.
10.   Thou shalt not covet thy neighbor's
house, thou shalt not covet thy neighbor's
wife, nor his manservant, nor his maidservant,
nor his ox, nor his ass, nor anything that is
thy neighbor's.
Please answer the following questions based on
our version of the Ten Commandments. But we
would also like your tradition's version of the
Ten Commandments if and where it differs from
ours.
These are the question on which Dr. Laura based
her new book - The Ten Commandments.

1. What role do the Laws of Noah have in your covenant with God?
2. Is there any connection between the Ten Commandments of the Old Testament and Jesus in the New Testament?
3. Why are the Ten Commandments more important than the other God given laws of the Old Testament and why are these other laws not binding?
4. If acceptance of Jesus as your savior is the essential element of Salvation, why are the Ten Commandments important?
5. If Salvation is dependent on accepting Jesus as the Savior, how can the Ten Commandments be encouraged for non-Christians?
6. If it is sufficient to believe in Jesus as Savior to achieve Salvation, then what is the motivation to observe the Ten Commandments?
7. Since the Ten Commandments were given before Christianity existed, how do Christians deal with the words of the first commandment which state "I am the Lord your God who brought you out of the land of Egypt"?
   a. If the phrase "who brought you out of the land of Egypt" is downplayed, what is the source of authority for the rest of the commandments?
8. According to your tradition what is exactly forbidden in the second commandment?
   a. How do you define a graven image? (i.e. is Sistine Chapel a graven image given that God is portrayed?)
9. According to your tradition what does it mean to swear falsely by God's name and how does this differ from blasphemy?
   a. If God does "not forgive" swearing falsely by his name how does one gain redemption?

10. How does your tradition define holy activities and behavior for the Sabbath?
a. What is permitted and what is forbidden?
b. Do you preach about not working or shopping on the Sabbath? (please explain)
11. How does your tradition define honoring thy mother and father?
a. What actions are mandatory and what actions are optional?
b. Are there any conditions under which you condone not honoring parents (for example, abandonment, abuse, molestation, parental infidelity)?
What is your interpretation of "and your days shall be lengthened"?
12. Do you see a distinction between murder and killing? If so, what is it?
a. Within your tradition is it permitted to terminate heroic medical measures?
b. Within your tradition are there any situations or conditions for which you could condone abortion? (explain)
c. Within your tradition are there any situations or conditions for which you could condone the death penalty?
d. How does this commandment impact your tradition's view of killing in war?
e. How does this commandment impact your tradition's view of self-defense or killing to save another's life in mortal danger?
13. What do you think is your congregation's general attitude toward adultery?
a. What rationalization have congregants given you to excuse their adultery?
b. Are there any conditions under which you could condone it (i.e. a chronically ill spouse or marital separation)?

c. Is there a communal stigma or punishment (i.e. shunning) for known adulterers in your congregation?

d. Do you ever advise adultery as grounds for divorce?

e. Would you officiate at the marriage of a couple whose relationship began as an adulterous one?

14. Are there any conditons under which your tradition condones stealing? (i.e. Robin Hood syndrome?)

15. What does "bearing false witness" mean to your tradition?

16. How do you explain "thou shalt not covet" to your congregation?

a. Does this include action and/or thoughts?

17. What is your religious affiliation? Training?

18. Are you/have you been clergy?

This is what people who read this book have to say!

The Ten Commandments

#1

Heaven is vacant and hell will be crammed full. I can never be this good. I pray that GOD is merciful and full of pity for me, a miserable sinner. As you read this book, keep in mind that Dr. Laura is all about being provocative and outrageous. That's what keeps her on the air. She's opinionated, but she will be the first to say so, and that's what people call her for. Take her with a grain of salt.

#2

I felt like a naughty child being scolded
by mommy dearest. About writing ability, I'm
not sure; but nerve is certainly not lacking in
this woman. Before you take moral/religious
counsel from Dr. Laura, ask her about many of
her own unfortunate personal choices. "You are
how you behave" (not how you pretend to). I
found Rabbi Vogel's input severly limited. Dr.
Laura should turn off her word processor and
microphone and go away. She should be ashamed,
but isn't capable.

#3

A book of self-righteous hypocrisy which
stretches the limits of moral fantasy.
Wouldn't it be great to live a life of Dr.
Laura? I think she needs a dose of reality of
what it takes to raise children. First of all,
income. I think it would be great to just stay
at home with the kids but it doesn't pay the
bills. I'd just like to ask Dr. Laura how much
quality time she spends with her children with
a three hour radio show, speaking engagements,
her book writing dealings, her impressive work
out regimen, etc. This is a book about
guarding the hen house written by Mr. Fox.

#4

Dr. Laura's been up on the mountain a
little too long and needs to come back down to
earth for a dose of reality. Yeah, wouldn't it
be great to stay home and raise the kids, but
unfortunately it doesn't pay the bills.
Wouldn't it be nice to be able to stay married

and live happily ever after, but get real. Growing up in a loveless home where parents are barely able to stand each other certainly isn't my idea of a role model family the kids should pattern themselves after. Dr. Laura lives in a Cinderella world but unfortunately the rest of us live in the real world where people make mistakes and the world is at times cruel.

#5

They always start the same way, don't they, as something that may be a bit extreme, in this case as a self-proclaimed "secular feminist". Then, after a pivotal epiphany, a one-eighty turnaround and maybe a crash course in counseling to borrow legitimacy for their pitch, they launch a new career of giving stridently rigid advice to anyone anguished and/or confused enough to ask for it. Eventually and inevitably, they consider themselves qualified to speak for God. Sad, isn't it?

#6 Do as I do, not as I did??????

That's a quote from "Dr." Laura – obviously she could and has broken quite a few of the 10 Commandments she so piously writes about. Most of what she pontificates about in both this book and on her radio show are things she did not do or did the opposite of in her own life. Stay at home mother? Not her. Pre-marital sex? Plenty of it when she found it useful. Before we start reading and listening to people like the doctor of physiology (which has nothing to do with psychiatry or theology) perhaps it would behoove us to know more about who is doing the preaching. This woman has no conscience. She is chasing the almighty dollar and if she has to use the Ten Commandments and the bible to it, she certainly doesn't care.

#7 When will she stop?

Not only is she an expert of bad behavior and the morals of the universe, but now she's written about the Ten Commandments! I can't believe the world has survived all this time without Dr. Laura. If you need guidance on the Bible, read one of the millions of books by scholars of the text. Better yet, go to your rabbi, priest or minister for their advice and maybe a few suggestions on good books to read.

#8 Makes a fantastic doorstop!

This book is the best doorstop you will ever find. Her ridiculous comments on "moral absolutes" are highly laughable even to a beginning logician. The best comedy read since Bob Dole's comedy. (a bowl of laughs…save for the notion that this book is serious about utter nonsense!)(end)

On October 27, 1998, Dr. Laura announced on her radio program that she would be starting a "Bible" study session on her web site where her listeners could participate in group discussions about the Bible. The strange part about this is she said the "Bible" study would be based on her new book, "The Ten Commandments". When did her book come to represent the "Bible?" Has she written the "NEW" Bible for the next 2000 years?

CHAPTER ELEVEN

DR. LAURA AS ENTERTAINMENT ONLY

I have taken Dr. Laura at face value for many years now. She is the equivalent of a Jerry Springer, Jenny Jones, and all the other talk shows that have bombarded our senses in the last few years. If you can see it as that, you will not get frustrated when you listen to her show. Here is how some of her listeners see her as an entertainer.

#1

Geez, some of you people really need to lighten up. Look...I'm not a Schlessinger fan; frankly, I despise the woman. But hey...It's entertainment. People tune in to laugh themselves silly at the pathetic people who call in. Contrary to the "concerns" of the bourgeois liberals who can't seem to understand, programs like this one are intended as...(gasp)...entertainment. And contrary to the afore-mentioned bourgeois types, most of us are in on the joke.

#2

I don't really understand the new conservatism of the heart. It seems, the children of the 60's, reaching middle age are embracing the idea that their parents lived in an ideal world in the 40's and 50's. The beautiful world when frigidity and impotence were considered virtues, and the joy of sexuality was the greatest sin. When men used prostitutes to compensate for their wives' society induced frigidity and their own ignorance, when parents hating each other stayed together for the "benefit of the children", their own fear of acting according to their needs and taking responsibility for their own actions.

What is Dr. Laura - except an over-inflated ego? Is she a therapist? Who did she cure? I don't see who would pay to be hurt by her abusive and rude stupidity. Could it be that her failure as a therapist made her choose a career as an entertainer?

Is she a role model? God fear us…Would you want Laura Schlessinger as your mother, or wife? What makes her so right? What makes her more right than any other person? She failed at her own first marriage and I have not heard her husband telling us how happy she makes him. Just because she's married gives her the MORAL RIGHT to abuse any mother who decides to work for a living.

Is she a sociologist? She does advocate her beliefs as ultimate truths, regardless of all the scientific evidence against them.

Is she a rabbi? If she was a rabbi and her show would have been a religious show, I would understand her rage at the nonbeliever and sinner (even if I don't agree with it). But to condemn everything you dislike and everybody that you don't agree with in the name of medical science, and use your medical degrees in the process, looks to me like medical malpractice. Society should not give her the right to practice psychotherapy in order to ridicule needy people in front of everybody. I feel offended by the way she treats and ridicules some callers and personally think that her license to practice psychotherapy should be suspended.

So a failed therapist, failed rabbi, failed sociologist, is wealthy, married, and is successful as an entertainer. What kind of entertainment? The entertainment of radio listeners at the expense and humiliation of most callers. The same kind of entertainment as Jerry Springer or Geraldo. This is what her therapy is all about.

#3

What I've noticed is she is totally inflexible and incredibly self-opinionated as if she is an expert on any and everything. The woman's ego must be bigger than the total sum of her listeners.

Add this: She doesn't really seem to listen to what the true message is from the caller. Many times she rudely cuts them off when she is able to quickly pigeon hole them within one of her pre-determined categories that all people fit within, no matter how unique their problem may be, that is if they are allowed to even identify it at all.

Dr. Laura is entertainment at best, and it's scary the way some of the poor misguided souls call in looking for a serious answer (fast fix) to a lifelong problem. She is bandstanding on the darker side of the popular ride and acceptance of Talk Radio.
Her introduction should be preceded by, "The

following show does not represent the views of this station, and are intended for entertainment purposes only".

#4

Dr. Laura openly invites people to call in to discuss their problems over the air. If you respond to Dr. Laura with the wrong answer or committed a wrongful act, you will be chewed out by Dr. Laura with no mercy. When you invite people over to your home, do you immediately chew them out for every mistake they committed since you last saw them? I understand she needs to keep her sponsors happy by maintaining her ratings. But does she need to mock strangers with real problems over the air and justify her actions as nagging. Is that professional behavior by a Doctor? Kinda reminds me of Jenny Jones show using sensationalism and people's misery to generate income and ratings. Maybe we should provide Dr. Laura with a referral to a real doctor - a doctor with empathy, sympathy, and sincere concern over people's problems.

#5

I am somewhat new to Dr. Laura's show, only having listened to about six programs. The first couple of shows I found her to be entertaining and insightful. The more I listened, the more disturbing her "insights" became.
When she called a grandmother a "slut" simply because she was living with a man outside of marriage, I had heard enough. What wisdom she may possess is lost amongst a

perverted sense of piety. How many decent, moral, hard working people like myself are to be vilified in the worst ways simply because we haven't committed our relationships on paper?

"Dr. Shitslinger" is merely Rush Limbaugh's female alter-ego, bombastic, judgemental, infallible and all too willing to lead her gullible listeners down the primrose path of a myopic morality long since proven false.

#6

I personally think Dr. Laura is a hoot. I agree with the concept of one's taking responsibility for one's life and actions but she takes it to an aggressive extreme.

Dr. Laura is about JUDGEMENT and GUILT. Sort of a 90's icon of those biddy nuns from Catholic school. I find neither of those areas particularly attractive, but witnessing her simultaneously slay some callers, and be idealized by others, for me is highly amusing. Like the Roman experience of tossing Christians to the lions, there is a primal urge satisfied hearing the sadistic "doctor" make waste of the wimpy approval seekers who call.

I find the rumors to her son's legitimacy the biggest hoot of all (is that TRUE???). But it's not a surprise. Look at the supreme list of hypocrisy in the cheerleader of ignorance, Rush Limbaugh.

I have respectively put together a modest list of To-Do's and Not-To-Do's when calling Dr. Laura, for those innocent lambs…
1. Do not with a straight face tell her you are living with your boyfriend and expect her to act like it's a good idea.

2. Do not call up because you want Dr. Laura to judge someone else in your life. She's in the business of judging YOU. You'll be mincemeat, honey.

3. Do lead with the bottom line first, if you don't, you'll be interrupted, analyzed and condemned before your real question is asked.

4. Do not declare yourself to be a member of a religious denomination unless you are fully prepared to live up to every precept of said religion.

5. Do not declare yourself to be married unless you are fully prepared to live up to every precept of said vows.

6. Do not with a straight face tell her that you are a mother with a job.

7. Do not tell her you are pregnant and single unless you have already gotten the adoption papers signed.

8. Do not brag to her about the cat you bought your teenager.

9. Do not allude to your children knowing that you have sex.

10. Dr. Laura is an Aquarius, which means that she never wants to be pigeon-holed...so if you are a right wing conservative thinker, you have this great advocate. Do not make any racial or anti-gay remarks. Your head will be handed quicker to you than you can say "Judge Not Lest You Shall Be Judged..."

#7

Although I have been a seven-day-a-week subscriber of my local newspaper for many years, I have recently changed my subscription to week-end only because the "Today" section recently began running a column by Dr.

Schlessinger every Thursday. Even though there are probably many articles and columns in the newspaper that I would find that I disagree with everyday, I find her column particularly offensive. I have heard her radio show and feel the same way.

It is my opinion that Dr. Schlessinger is an extremist. As with all extremist, in her version of a perfect world, her views would make perfect sense. In her world, every person would be responsible for their actions. Fathers and mothers would always be married, and always bring their children up well. Spouses wouldn't divorce each other. Non-married persons wouldn't have sex at all. Women with children would not have jobs. If this was the way the world was, then her views would make perfect sense. But it's not. And it never will be. The most we can hope for is that each person is responsible to and for themselves, and prioritizes things in their life, their loved ones, careers, and personal time to the best balance possible.

One thing that particularly bothers me is how seriously many people take her. Other "ridiculous" public personalities, such as Rush Limbaugh, Howard Stern, and the like, have far-out views that are not practical, but for the most part people realize this and don't take them very seriously. In fact, although I don't agree with nearly all the views of these particular people, I get a kick out of reading and listening to them, purely for entertainment value! And chances are, these people probably do not take themselves that seriously! But Dr. Laura Schlessinger, on the other hand, takes herself and her views very seriously, and feels that anyone who does not subscribe to her EXACT beliefs is, in her words, a "bum" or a "slut".

Moralistic preaching will not have a permeating effect on anyone but those who already believe the way she does. Kindness and compassion can and does change the lives of many people. Dr. Schlessinger sorely lacks these traits.

#8

Dr. Laura takes advantage of her callers, some of them with real problems and she is rude and abusive. Her ideas are stupid, unscientific and her manner is offensive.

More recently she is making that stupid kid into some kind of therapist also. What makes her ideas about the world in general better than everybody else's?

As far as I am concerned her show is of the same kind as Rikki Lake's and Jerry Springer's. Just a clever way of making money by taking advantage of some, through exposing their misfortune for the entertainment of many. What revolts me more is that Laura uses the title "doctor" in order to do this. What scares me is her popularity with a public that now believes that the 60's were all sin and the 50's virtue...

#9 It's Showtime!

The Dr. Laura show is nothing more than entertainment at it's lowest form - on the same level as the sleazy T.V. shows like Jerry Springer and Sally Jesse. These shows, the books and all the other crap surrounding these people, exist and survive for one reason; our society loves to watch the sucker get roasted.

The Dr. Laura show revolves around a well-planned "checklist" which is adhered to rigidity. The caller is basically steered down a narrow corridor that has only one door. If the caller hesitates or questions the doctor's position, they are subjected to a vicious thrashing. The first rule on the "checklist" is "never question the queen's authority".

Laura Schlessinger is nothing more that an opportunist on the grandest scale. The question regarding her credentials is really not the issue. Someone with a mail-order diploma and a sharp tongue with the willingness to "beat the sucker mercilessly" could do the job as well. What is amazing is the seemingly endless supply of guilt-ridden people that feel they simply have to step into the good doctor's confessional and then allow her to dole out the penance. If this show were done with a studio audience, there would be a bunch of misfits cheering at the top of their lungs as the doctor whips the poor dummies into submission before telling them to "take on the day". It is both sad and comical, but most important – it sells big time.

The other misconception people have is that this woman is a right wing conservative. I believe she would jump the fence in a heartbeat if the grass were greener on the other side. She is a capitalist, pure and simple. What self-respecting conservative would trot out "the children" more times than Ted Kennedy and Hillary Clinton combined? After the "flap" in Dallas, I believe she said she was donating the proceeds of the event to unwed mothers. Now let's see here. These are the same women she labels "sluts" on her show. She tells them they

deserve no sympathy for their irresponsible
behavior, but now she is going to reward them.
Or is that for "the children"? Yup! Yup! She's
conservative all right.

If she were offered a cabinet position in
the Clinton Administration she would grab the
power in an instant. I'd kind of like to see
that. I doubt if she could bullshit the senate
committee the way she does her callers. As she
discovered in Dallas, you can't fool all of the
people all of the time. Especially when you're
not on your throne in the studio.

#10

Dr. Laura and Rush Limbaugh have much in
common. Both have a limited grasp of issues and
lack the educational and professional
background to back up their inflammatory and
hurtful opinions. It's all about money for both
of them.

I imagine the two of them to be socially
inept geeks who have finally at this late point
in their lives found an outlet to get back at
all the people who have snubbed them in the
past. Laura and Rush are perfect for radio
venues that allow no issue to be discussed for
more than 60 seconds and allow for no free
flowing discourse between listeners and DJ.
Both Laura and Rush would not hold up for more
than 60 seconds in any honest interview.

I will say that Rush is easier to take
because I sense he knows he is an entertainer
and not much more. Laura seems like she
actually believes her hype.

Also, what is a degree in Physiology used
for?

#11

I listen to Dr. Laura mainly for amusement, although I have to tune out for long periods because her manner is so horribly offensive.

I really have to wonder what her problem with feminists, and women in general could be. If it weren't for the Women's movement, would she be anywhere but barefoot and pregnant in the kitchen? Would she have had the opportunity to become as highly educated as she claims to be? There is something highly suspicious about a woman who has such a deeply rooted hatred of other women. Perhaps she just lacks character. That would be my guess.

Why does she and others like her have such a fear of liberals? It's because we think for ourselves. Religion is a means of gaining control over a population, and good liberals like myself don't feel the need to pore through the Bible or talk to a priest every time we have a problem. We are a threat to the religious establishment because we don't NEED religion to live happy, productive lives.

Dr. Laura finds the liberal establishment threatening because we do not support her empire. We don't buy her books and other trinkets, line up to get her autograph or wait breathlessly on the line to announce "I am my kid's mom!" She won't get rich off people who have the ability to run their lives without her input.

#12

As a REAL licensed Ph.D. type clinical psychologist, with twenty years' experience, I am very troubled by Dr. Laura's apparent

inability to recognize florid psychopathology
in her callers. Clearly, 30 to 60 seconds of
moralizing is not going to do anything other
than create guilt over what these needy
individuals are unable to change, except with
considerable help and motivation. It appears to
me that "Dr." Laura is more similar to the
Jerry Springer's than a serious therapist such
as Joy Brown. I truly wish she were not on the
air as I do not feel in general that she is
helping anyone.

DR. LAURA'S CREDENTIALS

#1 Howard Stern talks about Dr. Laura on his October 20, 1998 show.

Dr. Laura is not even a medical doctor. She's a GODDAMN GYM TEACHER in PHYSIOLOGY! Gym teachers are the dumbest teachers in school! They are even dumber than a shop teacher, because at least a shop teacher can measure things. The only reason why she is popular is because she MENTIONS MY NAME.

#2

I have been following this so-called doctor with some amusement and alarm. My comments may be helpful to your readers in terms of understanding Dr. Laura. I am a therapist and an attorney. I am in the process of becoming a Licensed Marriage and Family Therapist. Many people have already noted that the 'doctor' that Dr. Laura sports is not in counseling or therapy, but in physiology, which has nothing to do with either counseling or therapy. So far as I know, the ethical codes of all counseling and therapy professions prohibit the use of credentials that do not relate to the profession. For example, even though I have a doctorate in law, my degree in counseling is a master's degree, so it would be unethical for me to bill myself as "Dr." in my counseling profession. Furthermore, it is my responsibility to correct the misimpression when people call me doctor, as they often do.

The reason for this is that it is wrong for professionals to mislead others about their credentials. Partly, it is to protect the public from being misled in their decisions about whom to trust to provide them with competent help. More important, it is to keep us professionals honest in our dealings with our clients and with other professionals.

When one is in the role of 'therapist', whether we like it or not that role takes on something of parenthood, certainly authority. In that role, what we model for our clients in our own behavior, and our own attitude toward them, is much more important than any 'advice' that we might give. It is the relationship that counts. By misrepresenting herself to the public, this woman is in effect saying to the public, and to her true believers, that it is okay to misrepresent yourself to people.

Furthermore, in her relationship with her callers, she is giving several other important messages:
1. It is okay to be mean, judgmental and nasty.
2. It is okay to not listen to others before forming an opinion.
3. A pithy comeback is more important than struggling with others through complex issues.
4. It is more important to prove that you are right than admit that you have made a mistake.
5. Image is everything, and as long as you look good (sound good) and say the right things, then what's inside doesn't matter.
I could go on. The point is that this so-called 'doctor' doesn't even use the skills that she ought to have learned in getting her master's degree. She doesn't listen and she lacks empathy.

#3

What's wrong with Dr. Laura? Here is a short list of highlights:

1. She allows people to assume her doctorate is in psychology. It is in physiology. She is a licensed marriage and family counselor, but this is not the same as a psychologist, and listeners should at least be made aware of this distinction.

2. She cuts people off and gives off the cuff advice for what could be serious problems deserving more discussion. This could lead callers to ineffective or damaging behavior.

3. She buys into the gender-based behavioral arguments. My being male says nothing about my specific behavior. These generalizations may hold for statistical averages in the population but ignore that they primarily derive from learned behavior from sterotypical role models. Each person is an individual and should be taken as such. (In fact, her aggressive style indicates more "masculine" behavior than I exhibit.)

4. She is ineffective at disguising her anti-homosexual bias. Saying that homosexuality is abnormal suggest dysfunctionality, even if she says that it's OK because they were born that way. Furthermore, her insistence that same-sex parents are automatically inferior to a mother and father situation (relying again on gender-based stereotypical assumptions) betrays her real attitude towards homosexuality. Again, each case needs to be looked at separately.

The bottom line is that psychological problems and relationship problems should be given sufficient time to ferret out just what the problem is with no preconceived biases on the part of the therapist. Perhaps the

licensing board should consider revoking her
license for taking such an irresponsible
approach to counseling.

#4

     My friend refuses to listen to Dr. Laura
for many reasons but when we debated this
recently, the point he kept returning to is
that she claims to be a doctor when she really
is not… I refuted every other argument except
this one, as I couldn't find any documentation
which says she is a doctor of anything. I don't
mind if she's not a doctor, but my friend says
"if you're not and say you are, aren't you
lying?" and I can't argue.

LAST CHAPTER

HUMOROUS STUFF

25 RULES FOR WOMEN

1. Learn to work the toilet seat: If it's up, just put it down.
2. Don't change your hair. Ever.
3. Don't make us guess.
4. If you ask a question you don't want an answer to, expect an answer you don't want to hear.
5. Sometimes, he's not thinking about you. Live with it.
6. He's never thinking about "The Relationship".
7. Get rid of your cat. And no, it's not different, it's just like any other cat.
8. Dogs are better than ANY cats. Period.
9. Sunday + Sports. It's like the full moon or the changing of the tides. Let it be.
10. Shopping is not everybody's idea of a good time.
11. Anything you wear is fine. Really.
12. You have enough clothes.
13. You have too many shoes.
14. Crying is blackmail. Use it if you must, but don't expect us to like it.
15. Your brother is an idiot.
16. Ask for what you want. Subtle hints don't work.

17. No, he doesn't know what day it is. He never will. Mark anniversaries.
18. Share the bathroom.
19. Share the closet.
20. Yes and No are perfectly acceptable answers.
21. A headache that lasts for 17 months is a problem. See a doctor.
22. Nothing says "I love you" like sex in the morning.
23. Foreign films are best left to foreigners.
24. Check your oil.
25. Don't give us 50 rules when 25 will do.

I have been calmly watching over all my children since the beginning. I have spoken to many over the centuries. Some of you have heard me. Some of you just think you have heard me. Some have written very moving things about me and others and have taken to themselves cults and followings that I do not personally claim... But that's okay if it makes you better children. I just hate it when you make claims about me and others that are just flat out wrong. What really angers me is the hatred you show in my name. I am who I am. Do not take that from me and change me to whom you want me to be. I allow you to be you. I allow everyone to be. Let's get that straight. There is a reason I haven't talked to anyone in a long time. There isn't a one of you that will get it right, so I am quiet. But for my sake, stop fighting over who I am. I am who I am.

DR. LAURA APOLOGIZES FOR NUDE PICTURES

For two weeks, Dr. Laura denied the fact that she posed for nude pictures. On November 3, 1998, Dr. Laura finally admitted that the pictures were of her. This was, of course, after her court case was denied and she couldn't keep the pictures from being shown on the Internet.

Here is the statement Dr. Laura released to the public the day after the court said the pictures were already a matter of public record.

"Friends, we're going to have a little talk."

"I was advised not to comment about the photos on the Internet until after a court hearing Nov. 2, so I've waited until now to respond. First, I want to say how deeply I appreciate the encouragement and the support over these past days from so many listeners. It has made a very difficult time easier, and I thank you from my heart.

"Many letters and faxes generously say how grateful you are that some of your own past actions are buried in merciful oblivion, that will never come to light. Would that I could say the same!

"However, it isn't news to my longtime listeners and to those who read my books that I have undergone profound changes over the course of my life, the most important of which is my journey from basically an athiest, to an observant Jew.

"In my 20's, I was my own moral authority. The inadequacy of that way of life is painfully obvious today.

"At the same time, my early experiences have taught me how much better it is to live by an objective and absolute standard of right and wrong, preferably a standard set by God. And that is the hard won wisdom I try to pass along to others as I preach, teach and nag every day on this program.

" I want though to take a moment to address a couple of specific allegations that are simply not true. Most importantly, 23 years ago when I was 28, I legally separated from my husband, filed for divorce in the state of New York, and moved to California.

"Subsequently, I had a relationship with a man who was both mentor and friend, a relationship that has never been a secret. I am mystified as to why - 23 years later - this 80-year-old man would do such a morally reprehensible thing.

"So, despite acute embarrassment, but with thanks for my strong religious beliefs, and the support of family friends and so many of you, I'm still here! And you'll find me here today, tomorrow, and the next day, for as long as you want to keep tuning in. I'll come back with your calls in a moment"

HOW TOUCHING!!

BIGGEST TURKEYS OF 1997 TAKE TACKY TASTE AWARD!

The Gossip Show and cyber-readers of E!
Online submitted candidates for 1997 Tacky Taste
Awards. They were swamped with letters about
celebrities who qualified as turkeys for bad
taste.

Tackiest of them all?

1. Dr. Laura Schlessinger.
When she read that she'd been nominated for
Tacky taste 1998, Schlessinger gave her
syndicated radio audience a directive that
would qualify for a Convoluted Logic Award.
She said she wanted to win because those
who would vote her tacky must be against
morals, values, ethics, religion and God.
We got thousands of responses, with
hundreds of Dr. Laura's followers repeating
her phrase like robots. "I am voting for
Dr. Laura Schlessinger because there is a
group in this country that thinks morals,
values, ethics, religion and God are
tacky."
        "She's a hypocrite … not on speaking
terms with her mother. Claudette of
Twentynine Palms, CA wrote, "Many people
disagree with her" – and Claudette knows,
she told us, because she has a Web page
called "Dr. Laura Is Wrong" that gets
between 200 and 300 hits a day.

This was my first time in print about Dr.
Laura. I told her it would not be my last.
Guaranteed!!! Hello, Dr. Laura!

You can find a portion of my web page in the back of this book!

When Dr. Laura discovered that she had been nominated for the Tacky Taste Award, she was livid. She immediately got on the air and directed her hoards of listeners to bombard the P.O. Box with votes for her. She exclaimed, "How dare these people compare me to the likes of Marv Albert and Mike Tyson." These were the second and third runner-ups for the award. "There is a small group of people out there who have it in for me and will do anything to put me down." Little does she know - WE ARE NOT A SMALL GROUP.

#1

Today on Dr. Laura's show she mentioned that she was nominated by the E! channel in their annual Tacky Taste Awards along with Marv Albert and Mike Tyson. This is something that shows no class on the E! channel part less Marilyn Beck or Stacy Smith but hey, if they want to be tacky and Dr. Laura wants to win this award, I thought I might reprint the information given by her today. Dr. Laura asked us to write or e-mail our vote for her to show our Morals, Values, Family Values, Ethics, Principles, etc. to: (address ommitted)

Good Luck Dr. Laura.

#2

Dr. Laura wants to win the Tacky person of the Year award in order that the award does not go to her criminal opponents. Anyone who is willing to vote for her should send their vote to: (e-mail address omitted)

#3

Dear Ms. Smith:

I heard the end of Dr. Laura's request to e-mail her nomination, so I am not sure what your motivation was to include her in your group of nominees. Please e-mail back with your reasons. While I certainly don't agree with all of Dr. Schlessinger's "teaching, preaching and nagging," I firmly believe than on a balance this world would be a much better place if we all listened, in all senses of the word. I know that I have done some "noble" things as a result of "listening" which I might otherwise not have.
If you truly believe that what she has accomplished is the "tackiest," then I must agree and nominate her for "Tackiest Personality of the Year."

#4

Just ran across the poll for the Tacky Taste Award and Dr. Laura is running 2nd to Ellen Degeneres. Check out the web site and vote for Dr. Laura!

#5 The Winner is Dr. Laura!

Congrats to Dr. Laura in winning Marilyn Beck's Tacky Taste Award.

We all did it. If you missed it in your local newspaper or did not go to E! web site here is the text as taken from E online. I hope I have not broken any copyright laws, but hey, if it's for the good of Morals, Values, God, Ethics etc., I'll take the blame.

It's that time: Turkey Day. Happy Thanksgiving to one and all, and a very special thanks to all of you who voted. We've been swamped with letters about celebs who qualify as gobblers in this year's menu of bad taste.

And for the first time in this contest's two-decade history, we have stuffing - ballot box stuffing. So, without further ado, we start off with the biggest turkey of them all:

Number 1! Dr. Laura Schlessinger: When she read she'd been nominated for Tacky Taste 1998, Schlessinger told her syndicated radio audience that she wanted to win, because those who would vote her tacky must be against morals, values, ethics, religion and God. We got thousands of responses, with Dr. Laura's followers repeating her phrase like robots.

Others countered with sentiments such as those expressed by F. M. of New Orleans, who accused her of "self-aggrandizement." Well Dr. Laura, you win. You get the tacky tiara…

DR. LAURA IS WRONG

DR. LAURA IS WRONG TO FORCE HER "OPINIONS" ON THE REST OF THE WORLD!!! DR. LAURA'S IDEAS ARE AS DEAD AS THIS PICTURE. HER THINKING IS ANTIQUATED AND IN THE PAST. THE PAST IS LONG GONE, NEVER TO RETURN AGAIN. HERE ARE MY OPPOSING "OPINIONS" OF SOME OF THE THINGS DR. LAURA HAS TO SAY. I'M SURE THERE ARE MANY OTHER "OPINIONS" TO THESE STATEMENTS.

HERE ARE SOME EXAMPLES OF THINGS THAT DR. LAURA HAS TO SAY:

TEN STUPID THINGS DR. LAURA TELLS WOMEN TO DO TO MESS UP THEIR LIVES!!

1. LIE TO YOUR TEENAGE DAUGHTER ABOUT THE FIRST TIME YOU HAD SEX. SHE TOLD A WOMAN TO LIE ABOUT WHEN SHE GOT MARRIED SO THAT HER DAUGHTER WOULD

NOT KNOW THAT SHE WAS PREGNANT WHEN SHE GOT MARRIED. HOW MANY TIMES HAS THAT HAPPENED?? IN THE FIRST PLACE, I DON'T THINK THAT A WOMAN SHOULD LIE TO HER DAUGHTER ABOUT ANYTHING. MANY WOMAN ARE PREGNANT WHEN THEY GET MARRIED. JUST BECAUSE IT HAPPENED TO THE MOTHER DOES NOT MEAN THAT IT WILL HAPPEN TO THE DAUGHTER BECAUSE SHE IS AWARE OF IT.

2. TELLS WOMEN TO LEAVE TOWN WHEN BEING THREATENED BY A MAN. WOMEN SHOULD LEARN TO DEFEND THEMSELVES, NOT RUN. IF WE KEEP RUNNING WE WILL ALWAYS HAVE THE PROBLEM. IF A MAN HITS A STRANGER ON THE STREET, HE CAN GO TO JAIL FOR ASSAULT. IF HE BEATS HIS WIFE OR THE WOMAN HE CLAIMS TO LOVE, THAT'S NOT A CRIME. THE LAWS NEED TO REFLECT THAT A WOMAN HAS THE RIGHT TO DEFEND HERSELF FROM THESE MANIACS. IF A MAN IS KILLED IN THE PROCESS, SO BE IT. IT SHOULD BE NOTHING MORE THAN SELF DEFENSE.

3. TELLS WOMEN NOT TO HAVE AN ABORTION, HAVE THE BABY AND PUT IT UP FOR ADOPTION. AS FAR AS I KNOW, ABORTION IS A LEGAL PROCEDURE IN THIS COUNTRY. IF DR. LAURA IS SO AGAINST ABORTION, I THINK THAT SHE SHOULD TAKE ALL OF THE BABIES THAT SHE SAYS SHOULD NOT BE ABORTED AND TAKE CARE OF THEM HERSELF.

4. NEVER SPANK A CHILD, THAT'S CHILD ABUSE. I SEE NO PROBLEM WITH CHILDREN GETTING SPANKED ON OCCASION. IT KEPT ME IN LINE WHEN I WAS GROWING UP AND IT PROBABLY KEPT HER IN LINE ALSO. MAYBE IF SHE HAD USED A LITTLE DISCIPLINE ON HER SON, HE WOULD NOT HAVE BURNED HER HOUSE DOWN OR SPRAY PAINTED HIS ROOM.

5. IT NOT RIGHT FOR PEOPLE TO LIVE TOGETHER BEFORE MARRIAGE. AS FAR AS I KNOW, CONSENTING ADULTS HAVE THE OPTION OF LIVING TOGETHER AS OPPOSED TO MARRIAGE IF THEY SO CHOOSE. IT IS NOT SHAMEFUL OR IMMORAL, IT'S AN ALTERNATIVE TO MARRIAGE. BEING AN ADULT IS ABOUT HAVING CHOICES.

6. TELLS WOMEN THAT IT IS NOT OK FOR THEIR CHILDREN TO GO TO DAY CARE. DAY CARE IS AN ALTERNATIVE THAT HAS BEEN USED FOR YEARS. EVERYONE CANNOT STAY HOME AND CARE FOR THEIR CHILDREN. DR. LAURA HAD THAT LUXURY, EVERYONE DOESN'T.

7. TELLS WOMEN IT IS NOT OK TO HAVE SEX BEFORE MARRIAGE. HOW DARE THIS WOMAN TAKE THAT POSITION. I SUPPOSE THAT SHE WAS A VIRGIN THE DAY SHE WALKED DOWN THE ISLE FOR THE FIRST TIME. AND HOW ABOUT HER SECOND HUSBAND? DID SHE NOT HAVE SEX WITH HIM UNTIL THEY WERE MARRIED? MY MOTHER HAD THIS SAYING "DO AS I SAY, NOT AS I DO"! I GUESS DR. LAURA LIVES BY THAT SAME SAYING.

8. TELLS WOMEN TO PASS UP A GOOD EDUCATION TO RAISE THEIR CHILDREN. A WOMAN SHOULD PURSUE WHATEVER SHE WANTS TO AND NOT FEEL GUILTY BECAUSE HER CHILDREN ARE IN SOMEONE ELSES CARE FOR A FEW HOURS A DAY.

9. TELLS WOMEN TO STAY IN A BAD MARRIAGE FOR THE KIDS SAKE. IT IS BETTER FOR

9. TELLS WOMEN TO STAY IN A BAD MARRIAGE FOR THE KIDS SAKE. IT IS BETTER FOR CHILDREN TO LIVE IN A HAPPY HOME WITH ONE PARENT THAN TO LIVE IN A HOME WITH TWO PARENTS WHO FIGHT ALL OF THE TIME.

10. TELLS WOMEN QUIT THEIR JOBS TO TAKE CARE OF THEIR KIDS NO MATTER WHAT FINANCIAL SITUATION IT WILL PUT THEM IN. MY KIDS LIKE TO EAT. THEY ALSO LIKE HAVING NICE THINGS. IT DOESN'T HURT THEM BECAUSE I AM GONE FOR A FEW HOURS A DAY TO PROVIDE FOR THEM. CHILDREN UNDERSTAND THAT PARENTS HAVE TO WORK.

THIS IS A LETTER I WROTE TO DR.
DR. LAURA,

I HEAR YOU ALL OF THE TIME TALKING ABOUT PEOPLE NOT BEING IN A COMMITTED RELATIONSHIP UNLESS THEY ARE MARRIED. YOU ARE WRONG AS YOU ARE ABOUT MANY THINGS. THE DEFINITION OF COMMITMENT IS: "THE STATE OF BEING BOUND EMOTIONALLY OR INTELLECTUALLY TO SOMEONE OR SOME COURSE OF ACTION". I DON'T SEE WHERE A MARRIAGE LICENSE MAKES WHAT YOU FEEL FOR ANOTHER PERSON MORE OR LESS OF A COMMITMENT.
YOUR MORAL IDEALOGY IS ASKEW. I DON'T KNOW WHERE YOU GET YOUR INFORMATION, BUT THERE HAS NEVER BEEN A TIME IN OUR SOCIETY WHEN WOMEN DID NOT HAVE BABIES WITHOUT BEING MARRIED AND THERE NEVER WILL. WHERE DO YOU THINK ALL OF THESE PEOPLE IN OUR AGE RANGE ARE COMING FROM WHO ARE LOOKING FOR THEIR REAL MOTHERS? IT WASN'T FROM AN IMMACULATE CONCEPTION. THERE HAS NEVER BEEN A TIME IN OUR SOCIETY WHEN PEOPLE DID NOT LIVE TOGETHER WITHOUT BEING MARRIED AND THERE NEVER WILL. THERE IS NOTHING WRONG WITH CONSENTING ADULTS DOING THIS. THEY ARE NOT SHAMEFUL OR IMMORAL AS YOU PREACH. THE MORAL CONCEPTS THAT YOU HAVE IN YOUR MIND ABOUT THIS HAS NEVER BEEN A REALITY, ONLY A THEORY THAT HAS NEVER WORKED. ALSO, THERE HAS NEVER BEEN A TIME IN OUR SOCIETY WHEN WOMEN DID NOT GO TO WORK AND LEAVE THEIR CHILDREN IN THE CARE OF OTHERS AND THERE NEVER WILL BE!!! I AM HAPPY THAT WE ARE NOT ALL BOUND BY YOUR SO CALLED RULES. I'M NOT AND I NEVER WILL BE.

FROM: E. O.
"IT IS NOT RELIGIOUS TO BE AS MEAN AS YOU ARE.
E. O.
RESPONSE:
I AM NOT MEAN. DR. LAURA HAS HER OPINION AND I HAVE MINE. THEY HAPPEN TO BE VERY DIFFERENT. DR. LAURA WANTS EVERYONE TO BE THE SAME. I'M FOR INDIVIDUALITY. WE WERE ALL BORN WITH DIFFERENT MINDS FOR A REASON. I THINK THAT EVERY ADULT HAS THE RIGHT TO MAKE THEIR OWN CHOICES AND DECISIONS IN LIFE. THERE ARE NO SET RULES FOR US TO LIVE BY (unless you want to be controlled by a lot of commandments that were written (by a man) for the sole purpose of controlling other people. I am amazed that so many people fall for it.) IF THERE WERE, WE WOULD HAVE THAT IDEAL SOCIETY THAT DR. LAURA CRAVES. IT WILL NEVER HAPPEN. IF THAT'S BEING MEAN, THEN I GUESS I AM MEAN. I'M JUST EXPRESSING MY "OPINION". WHO ARE YOU ANYWAY E. O.? ERNESTEO PERHAPS. I HAVE SHOWN MYSELF. SHOW YOURSELF AND

STOP TRYING TO SHIELD DR. LAURA FROM THE TRUTH. SHE IS WRONG!! LIKE I SAID BEFORE, I AM NOT GOING AWAY. I AM HERE FOR THE DURATION. I AM A VERY POWERFUL FORCE TO BE DEALT WITH. CAN YOU HANDLE THAT? BY THE WAY, I AM NOT RELIGIOUS. YOU CAN'T PULL THAT CRAP ON ME.
CLAUDETTE

THIS IS ANOTHER LITTLE TIDBIT I SEND TO DR. LAURA EVERY NOW AND THEN TO REMIND HER THAT IT IS NOT HER PLACE TO JUDGE OTHERS. IF SHE BELIEVES IN GOD SO MUCH, WHY DOESN'T SHE FOLLOW HIS "ADVICE"?
IS IT WISE TO CRITICIZE YOUR NEIGHBOR WHO HAS A SPECK IN HIS EYE - ESPECIALLY WHEN YOU CAN'T BE SURE YOU DON'T HAVE A BEAM OF YOUR OWN?
MATTHEW 7:1 JUDGE NOT, THAT YE BE NOT JUDGED!!
DURING HIS LONG TRAVELS, JESUS OFTEN POINTED OUT THAT PEOPLE WHO THINK HIGHLY OF THEMSELVES ARE NO BETTER THAN ANYONE ELSE. IN FACT, JUST THE OPPOSITE IS TRUE. HE CONTINUALLY DREW PEOPLE'S ATTENTION TO THE FAITH OF SIMPLE, INNOCENT PEOPLE WITH PURE HEARTS. HE ALSO CAME ACROSS JEALOUS, BITTER PEOPLE WHO WERE ALWAYS EAGER TO JUDGE THEIR FAMILIES AND AQUAINTANCES. HE THOUGHT SUCH BEHAVIOR WAS WRONG FOR TWO REASONS. WHEN WE SPEND OUR TIME CRITICIZING OTHERS, WE OFTEN FORGET ABOUT CHANGING FOR THE BETTER OURSELVES. AND IF WE REALLY LOVE PEOPLE, WE DON'T FOCUS ON ALL THEIR IMPERFECTIONS. JESUS KNEW VERY WELL THAT WE ALL HAVE OUR FAULTS. THAT IS WHY HE SAID, "DON'T JUDGE OTHERS AND YOU WILL NOT BE JUDGED." HE ALSO KNEW THAT WHEN WE NITPICK ABOUT OTHER PEOPLE'S LITTLE IMPERFECTIONS, WE DON'T NOTICE OUR OWN BIG FAULTS. HE SAID, "FIRST TAKE THE BEAM OUT OF YOUR OWN EYE; THEN YOU WILL SEE CLEARLY TO BE ABLE TO HELP YOUR NEIGHBOR GET THE SPECK OUT OF HIS." HE TAUGHT US THAT SINCE WE ARE NOT PERFECT, WE SHOULDN'T JUDGE OTHERS. IT TAKES ALL OF THE ATTENTION AND ENERGY WE HAVE JUST TO CHANGE OURSELVES FOR THE BETTER.

DR. LAURA SAYS THAT SELF GRATIFICATION IS A BAD THING. IF YOU ARE NOT ALLOWED TO GRATIFY YOURSELF, I DON'T KNOW WHO IS?

DR. LAURA SAYS THAT PEOPLE HAVE TO ARGUE TO HAVE A GOOD RELATIONSHIP. WELL, MY HUSBAND AND I NEVER ARGUE. IF WE DISAGREE ABOUT SOMETHING, WE MEET IN THE MIDDLE OR AGREE TO DISAGREE, BUT WE NEVER ARGUE. BY THE WAY, WE HAVE A GREAT RELATIONSHIP.

I HEARD DR. LAURA TELL A WOMAN THAT ASKED FOR HER ADVICE ABOUT HER ELDERLY FATHER TAKING HER CHILDREN OUT FOR THEIR BIRTHDAYS (he has a heart condition and she was concerned that he might have a heart attack with one of her kids in the car) TO "RENT A LIMO." THE WOMAN SAID "EXCUSE ME"...AND DR. LAURA REPEATED "RENT A LIMO." THE WOMAN EXPLAINED THAT HER FAMILY WAS NOT IN A FINANCIAL POSITION TO "RENT A LIMO". NOW THAT SHE MAKES A LOT OF MONEY, SHE HAS FORGOTTEN THAT EVERYONE CAN NOT AFFORD TO "RENT A LIMO." I HOPE THAT SHE CAN REMEMBER A TIME WHEN THAT THOUGHT WOULD HAVE NEVER ENTERED HER MIND. SHE HAS RISEN HIGH ABOVE THE PEOPLE THAT LISTEN TO HER SHOW. "EARTH

TO DR. LAURA - COME IN PLEASE".

DR. LAURA IS ALWAYS TALKING ABOUT PEOPLE BEING RESPONSIBLE FOR THEIR OWN ACTIONS. SHE SAID A WOMAN SHOULD BE IN JAIL FOR MURDER BECAUSE HER DAUGHTER DIED FROM BEING OVER 600 POUNDS. WHERE IS THE DAUGHTER'S RESPONSIBILITY IN THIS SITUATION? SHE IS THE ONE WHO ATE THE FOOD. WHEN I WAS A CHILD, I WAS SPANKED FOR NOT EATING ALL OF THE FOOD ON MY PLATE. WHEN I WAS FULL, I REFUSED TO EAT ANYMORE. THIS GIRL MADE THE CHOICE TO OVEREAT. DR. LAURA NEEDS TO MAKE UP HER MIND. EITHER YOU ARE RESPONSIBLE FOR YOUR ACTIONS OR SOMEONE ELSE IS RESPONSIBLE FOR YOUR ACTION. WHICH IS IT?

DR. LAURA ON ATHIEST:
DR. LAURA STATES THAT ATHIESTS HAVE NO SOULS. SHE STATES THAT ATHIESTS CANNOT BE GOOD PEOPLE BECAUSE THEY HAVE NOTHING TO BASE GOODNESS ON. SHE STATES THAT ATHIEST HAVE NO CHARACTER AND THAT THEY WILL BURN IN HELL BECAUSE ATHIEST ARE THE ANTICHRIST. SHE STATES THAT ATHIEST ARE ROOTLESS AND DON'T KNOW HOW TO LOVE OR FEEL COMPASSION FOR OTHERS BECAUSE ALL OF THESE FEELINGS ARE CONNECTED TO A HIGHER POWER. IN HER OPINION EVERYONE SHOULD BE PART OF A "FLOCK" AND FOLLOW THE COMMANDMENTS OF SOME ORGANIZED RELIGION. SORRY - I AM NOT A SHEEP.

"QUOTES" FROM DR. LAURA
"AT WHATEVER AGE YOU START SMOKING MARIJUANA, YOUR BRAIN DOES NOT PROGRESS PAST THAT AGE".

"I DON'T GIVE ADVICE. I PREACH, TEACH, AND NAG TRYING TO GET PEOPLE TO FACE REALITY." WHO'S REALITY? HERS? I THINK SHE SHOULD JOIN US HERE IN THE REAL WORLD AND STOP TRYING TO GET PEOPLE TO REGRESS INTO THE PAST.

"IF A PARENT IS NOT TELLING THE TRUTH, YOU'RE NOT GOING AGAINST THAT PARENT. YOU'RE GOING AGAINST A LIE. AND YOU ALWAYS SHOULD DO THAT NO MATTER WHO IT COMES FROM. YOU SHOULD NEVER STAND BY A LIE JUST BECAUSE YOU WANT TO STAND BY THE PERSON TELLING THE LIE." "WOW" I HEARD THIS WOMAN TELL A LADY TO LIE TO HER DAUGHTER ABOUT BEING PREGNANT WHEN SHE GOT MARRIED. I GUESS IN HER "OPINION" IT IS THAT IT OK TO LIE ABOUT SOME THINGS SOMETIMES AND NOT OK TO LIE ABOUT OTHER THINGS AT OTHER TIMES. I DON'T GET IT!!

"ANYTHING YOU HAVE TO RUN FROM IS YOUR MASTER. IF YOU WANT TO BE A SLAVE TO YOUR FEARS OF INADEQUACY IN HANDLING THESE QUESTIONS, YOU WILL DRIVE YOURSELF NUTS." I GUESS WHEN YOU RUN FROM A MAN THAT IS THREATENING YOU, HE IS YOUR MASTER. ACCORDING TO DR. LAURA, RUN FROM YOUR MASTER LADIES, RUN. I SAY, "BUY A GUN LADIES, AND PROTECT YOURSELF."

PLEASE LEAVE YOUR COMMENTS ABOUT DR. LAURA AT MY E-MAIL ADDRESS MSPEARL@CCI-29PALMS.COM. I WOULD LIKE YOUR COMMENTS ABOUT DR. LAURA'S

PHILOSOPHY AND THE "ADVICE" SHE GIVES TO LISTENERS. IT DOESN'T MATTER WHETHER YOU AGREE OR DISAGREE. I WILL ADD ALL COMMENTS TO MY WEBPAGE.

COMMENTS

From: David Allen
Finally!!!!!.....An opposing view. I was getting tired of beating myself. The righteous one's act has gotten very old to me. Unfortunately, many people seem to be riding the wave. I am very leery of simplistic answers. Every situation is unique and has to be evaluated on its own merit. I'm also uncomfortable with people who deal in absolutes.
I would be interested to hear any comments, particularly counter points to Laura's one sided views.
There are two positions held by Laura that I cannot accept:
1. Divorce is not acceptable when kids are involved. In the best interests of the child, the parents should stay together regardless of whether they love each other or not. I can't for the life of me see how two miserable parents that have no respect for each other would benefit the child.
2. Children of divorce are basically doomed. Shared parenting by divorced parents and blended families only cause problems for the child. I don't buy that either. It may create a mountain of problems, but I believe single parent and blended families can work without children suffering.
Response:
I agree with you fully.

From: John
Is it only me, or is she snippy and condescending to some callers? True, many callers are either not willing to be truthful to Dr. Laura or themselves, but should she be downright rude? I think not.

From: Tim
I think Dr. Laura is snippy—even downright rude--to some callers. Sometimes this is deserved, either because the caller won't get to the point, or is not answering her questions, or is obviously trying to cover up his complicity in the problem he called about; but other times it is not. It seems to me that the incidence of undeserved rudeness by Dr. Laura has increased in the past couple of years. I don't know why this might be, although one obvious possibility is that success is going to her head a bit.

From: pritchard@empnet.com Jonathan Pritchard - Just found your website and I think its great. Yesterday, I wrote and sent off a letter to our local radio station that has Dr. Laura on for three hours a day. I wrote that I would not be listening to their station in the future because I can't stand Dr. Laura's constant religious preaching. We have a local religious station here that would be appropriate for her show. I also wrote that her laugh reminded me of someone's fingernails on a blackboard (cheap shot, but I couldn't resist). IF WE ALL LIVED LIKE DR. LAURA, WHAT A BORING TIRESOME WORLD THIS WOULD BE!
Response: Thank You Jonathan. I feel the same way.

From: hillary
You're right. I am afraid that she does more harm than good. I am especially concerned with her attitude towards "false memory" of child molestation. Folks have a difficult enough time with that issue without hearing on the radio, without having family and friends receiving "advice" from a person with the word "doctor" in front of her name. Hey, I did not know that her son burned down the house and spray painted his room....how did that happen when she was ALWAYS there with him being his mom? thanks for the time to make your page!
Response: You're right. She does do more harm than good.

From: Catherine
I find myself turned off by Dr. Laura's manner many times and lately I find myself going back and forth between another female psychologist that is on at the same time in our area.

From: Ed

Is Dr. Laura obnoxious? Sure. In some ways. She has her bad days. I've heard her when things aren't going well. But tell me, what is more obnoxious, someone who calls it like they see them, or someone who doesn't want to step on anyone's toes, who wants to make everyone their friend, or who won't tell you that you need to straighten up? While I do not like to get a swift kick in the butt that often, sometimes I need it, and it does me good. I may call the kick obnoxious, but at least I'm getting it.

From: May

Do you think it is polite to interrupt someone while they are talking, while they are trying to explain and make clear a position they hold but about which they have questions or doubts? Is it polite to take up a gauntlet in the midst of another's platform, and then proceed to carry your own gauntlet instead of giving the attention to the one who held it first?

What would you do if someone interrupted you and began to ask so many questions that you began to wonder what the original problem even was!!

Would you become so confused that the perfectly normal train of thought that you began with would become like a large platter of scrambled eggs, all messed up???? Would you like to be asking for assistance, trying to get YOUR point understood, and the person to whom you were speaking goes off on their own tangent, albeit in the same area but in a different direction?

There is only ONE judge and HE will be the one to tell all of us what we have done wrong. Dr. Laura has no authority to invoke her own beliefs on people. Advice is different, that can be taken or ignored. Her radio show is a very interesting model to which to listen. It illustrates the perfectly rude behavior of an intelligent, witty woman. When someone phones her for help, they evidently are desperate or they would go to their local Mental Health Association.

She should study one of her shows, just one time, with an open, accepting mind. Everyone can learn something from their own mistakes.

From: Eric

According to the divorce rate amongst Orthodox Jews, getting married at a YOUNG age is a good idea. I wish Dr. Laura would stop telling everyone to wait just because the statistics in the public at large speak against young marriages. Jewish philosophy says just the opposite (provided they are living in a truly Jewish Observant lifestyle...

From: Michael

I am a faithful Dr. Laura listener. I generally agree with her opinions. BUT!! today there was a caller who asked for her opinion if she should marry a man who has different beliefs in god!! You emphatically told her she should find a mate within her religion. I find this unbelievable!! If I followed this advise I would not be married to a woman that I dearly LOVE, have loved for 13 years, and will love till the end of my human life. We are parents of 3 beautiful daughters that we share our lives with. I am proud to say that I am my kids dad. We raise our children properly with emphasis on morality and principles and religiously. Both beliefs can be taught if you explain in straight forward english. I am proud of my family, and hate to think what I would have missed out on if I followed her advice.

From: anonymous

I agree with you 100%. Very well said. I'm glad there's at least one person who is able to think. Thank you for your input. I very rarely hear anything I agree with.

From: Mar

I'm a Dr. Laura nightmare: knocked up at 26 by a man married to someone else.

My poor, neglected, unfortunate kid is 5, has been reading since he was three and works 4 figure addition and subtraction.

He's already an orange belt in martial arts and sings solo in the church children's choir. He can discuss with you the importance of having a faith, patience and being able to forgive. He is a generous, kind-hearted child of God.

He graduated preschool with honors and has interpersonal skills that enable him to settle dsiputes among peers, apologize to them when he is guilty of a 5-year old fit of anger/tantrum and interact gracefully with children from ages 2 to 17. (My house is full of neighborhood kids often - boys and girls)

In his head are the telephone numbers to my office, cell phone, home phone, my mother's work phone and home phone.

He recognizes that there are consequences to choices and when he makes a bad one, he's got to face the music.

I could go on about him, but I'll spare you.

I returned to work when he was 3 months old. I had to since I was guilty of non-marital sex as well as adultry and opted to raise my child instead of choosing the noble act of adoption. I had to fight for child support but the sperm donor has not been a participant.

Yes, my son craves male attention, enough of which he does not receive from my dad, uncle, and brother-in-law, his godfather. I'm not ignorant of the fact that he would greatly benefit from a father's daily influence. I'd happily be home for him when he's done with his kindergarten day if I could be. The circumstances I made for myself preclude that ability. This semester he is in karate class while I attended graduate school.

Working moms vs. stay at home moms, marital child bearing vs. out of wedlock pregnancy--these are valid controversies. I'm making the best of my situation as are most of us. I've repented for my sins and live with my choices. It's difficult to raise children in the best of circumstances..Those of us who are not in the ideal situations don't need debate.

From: Lynn

I have been wanting to write in for ages to point out that the "stay at home mom" is a very recent trend. My father talks with great admiration about his grandmother spending her day working the farm side by side with his grandfather. Their oldest daughter took care of the house and other kids. And grandma reports that the minute these kids were big enough to hold a hoe, they were out working too! What? No infant stimulation programs? No mom continually doting-making them feel like the center of the universe? There wasn't time. Of course, all six of my great-grandmother's children grew into hard-working, productive adults. Amazing.

From: Margret

We live in economically volatile times. Downsizing, strikes etc. A family with only one income puts themselves at tremendous risk unless thay have a tremendous savings account. It often takes a downsized individual a year or more to find comparable work. Meanwhile, someone who has been out of the work force often needs retraining or recertifying and can't jump back in on a minute's notice. True, one can bag groceries and earn enough to eat but health insurance is tremendously EXPENSIVE. If you have little children, going without this insurance for any length of time is irresponsible. Relying on the government, extended family, etc., when you have refused to work, is unfair. My husband and I both work and have a comparable but modest, incomes. Our budget is set uo so.that we live on only one income. This way, a job loss means we could meet our regular bills as usual. We will continue to provide this measure of security for our family. Financial problems are the leading cause of divorce. We owe our children intact families.

From: Mike

I am not a religious person. To be frank, I do not believe there is a God and that all religion is based on man's (and woman's) need to understand the un-understandable and cope with not being able to accept one's non-existance.

However, I believe I am a much more moral person than the vast majority of people. I am the kind of person that would not hesitate to return a wallet full of money to it's rightful owner. I have a very strong sense of right and wrong. The dilema is how to impart my value system on my children in a non-religious way. I have come to realize that my litmus test of what is right is to extrapolate an action into the gross proportion of it being done by everyone. If everyone shoplifted, think what stores would be like. No merchandise to touch and inspect and unpleasant security measures. Other thoughts are equally valid. Cheating on tests and taxes, not following the law when no one is around, not helping someone in distress, not giving to charities, not smiling in public and generally being nice to strangers, not voting, not being informed or educated, supporting smut and other degenerate activities, buying stolen merchandise, etc. Obviously, the list goes on forever. I have found that applying this test to everything has guided me to always do what's right for society, my family and myself. I have exposed both of my children to religion and one is a faithful member of the church and the other thinks religion is a crock and wants nothing to do with it. I can, however, truly state that there is no difference in either child's values. Each has the same strict standards of honesty and right and wrong as myself.

EPILOGUE

So what do I hope you've gotten out of this book? Simple. I hope that it has helped you to understand that you are smart enough, strong enough, and have the ultimate power to make life decisions without the help of Dr. Laura, a "physiologist", who uses other people's pain and misfortune to further her popularity and make herself rich.

Recently, it has come to light many things in Dr. Laura's past that should make many of her listener's reconsider how they think about the doctor's advice. Her lack of communication with her family, the fact that she has done all of the things she preaches, teaches, and nags others not to do and she took nude pictures that showed up on the Internet. She advises women to lie, treats people like crap, and calls women "sluts" "hussy" and "stupid". She uses terms like "knocked up", "horny", and "screwing" on the air. Is this the type of person you want to guide you through life?

People make a lot of mistakes in life. That is how we learn. We should not be judged by someone who has made just as many mistakes as the rest of us, but has put herself up on a pedestal. Well, that pedestal has been chipped away and she has tumbled back down to earth with the rest of us, where she should have been the entire time.